natural connections

natural
connections

exploring northwoods nature
through science and your senses

EMILY M. STONE

Green Darner Media
Cable Natural History Museum

Natural Connections: Exploring Northwoods Nature through Science and Your Senses

Cover design: Kathi Dunn, dunn-design.com
Interior production: Dorie McClelland, springbookdesign.com

ISBN: 978-0-9972061-2-8

Second printing, 2017

Cable Natural History Museum Mission
Connecting people to Northwoods nature through educational experiences that inspire wonder, discovery, and responsibility.

Cable Natural History Museum Vision
We will be a trailhead, community hub, and regional destination with universal appeal. We inspire people toward stewardship of the environment and improve their lives.

Green Darner Media
Green Darner Media is an imprint of the Cable Natural History Museum. Its mission is to connect people to Northwoods nature through publications and other media that inspire wonder, discovery, and responsibility.

To All My Family

Lois Nestel

When we try to pick out anything by itself,
we find it hitched to everything else in the Universe.

John Muir

Contents

FALL

WINTER

Jenni Thomson

Preface

When I arrived at the Cable Natural History Museum in January of 2011, snowy ski trails greeted me warmly. I reunited with old friends from my Northland College days at every turn, and my parents enjoyed driving from Iowa to visit me, instead of flying halfway across the country. As the snow melted and the Namekagon River became canoeable, I felt like I'd arrived home. The Northwoods has called to me since my first trip to the Boundary Waters Canoe Area Wilderness, and it is up here, during college, where I began deepening my understanding of nature. Seeing wolf tracks, smelling white clouds of serviceberry flowers, paddling on crystal-clear rivers, squishing through bogs, and listening to loons wail through the wee hours of the night feel like essential parts of my daily life. I am grateful to be here.

When I arrived at the Museum, I inherited a legacy of excellent natural history education and a big responsibility to continue it into the future. One of the ways that the Museum carries out its mission is by providing local newspapers with weekly natural history articles. Lois Nestle, the Museum's founding director and first naturalist, called her delightful column "Wayside Wanderings." When Lois retired in 1990, Susan (Benson) Thurn began to write about seasonal events in "Nature Watch." In 2011 it became my job to pick a new name for the column and begin writing.

I'd been toying with the idea of connections for several years as I taught science camp in the redwoods, watched wolves in Yellowstone, and studied "landscape interpretation" at the University of Vermont. As I moved from seasonal jobs to outdoor adventures back and forth across the country, my connections to people and places kept me grounded. So, the name Natural Connections came, well, naturally.

The writing came naturally, too. I grew up as a voracious reader and dabbled in writing stories throughout my childhood. In high school, my dad (a journalist) and my mom (his proofreader) edited my writing assignments with a generous dose of red pen. Besides the normal grammar and punctuation corrections, Dad would ask, "Are you sure this is the word you want?" "Is there a better way you can say that?" "What exactly do you mean here?" Mom and Dad still proofread my articles every week, no matter how close I cut the deadline.

Turning out a new essay each week, on top of the rest of my teaching and planning responsibilities, is never easy. But then, the most valuable things in life never are. The benefits have been immeasurable. For one, I love having someone to share my excitement with as seasonal changes bring old friends out of hiding, or when I discover an unusual phenomenon. I also relish having the excuse to learn something new. While a few articles are based solely on recent experiences or knowledge already in my head, during most weeks I do a fair amount of research into my topic. In this way I'm truly standing on the shoulders of giants. Google Scholar has been an amazing resource for finding out the latest scientific research and picking up on facts that are not widely known, even among other naturalists.

Perhaps one of the most interesting benefits of writing these weekly essays is that I've been forced to see the world a little differently. I don't always have as much time to spend outside as I'd like, and as seasons drag on, it can be hard to see something new to write about. I've had to learn how to turn the simplest things—like encountering a spider during my morning yoga, seeing the stars on a late drive home from a program, weeding my garden, or even being bit by insects—into stories worthy of your interest and connected to the world. What that has taught me, in the end, is that the opportunity for nature connection is all around us, all the time. Going on a hike is wonderful, but so is observing the invertebrates around your house.

I hope that this book serves at least two purposes. First, I'd like to help transport you into the woods with me, where we can experience and learn about the beautiful Northwoods together. Second, I'd like to inspire you to look a little closer and discover your own natural connections wherever you are.

Emily M. Stone
Cable, Wisconsin

SPRING

Look to the Sky

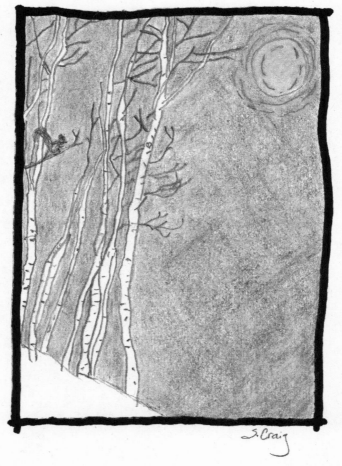

Stacy Craig

Crusty snow crunched loudly under my skis as I powered up a hill. My arms burned as I compensated for the chunky, uneven, spring snow. All my concentration focused down on the gray snowpack and inside my core.

Then I reached the crest of the hill and looked up. Blue sky and bright sun filtered through every gap in the trees. My mood lifted.

I am a naturalist, not a philosopher or religious scholar, but it seems to me that in both religion and nature we look to the sky for assurance that rebirth will occur. In springtime especially, prayerful folks are lifting their eyes skyward to thank a higher power for a certain ancient resurrection. When the world around us is gray and cold, and it seems like spring might never come, a look to the sky reassures us. That deep, blue color; the lengthening days; and the intensity of the sun all signal that the ancient rebirth of spring, however slow, is on its way.

Earlier last week, damp cold permeated the silent woods. Dark trees stood somberly, the live ones indistinct from the dead. I trudged on in melancholy monotony. Suddenly I became aware of my mood and the tunnel of gray that had ensnared me. To break free, I looked to the sky and felt hope return.

During these gray days of early spring, when food is scarce for many in nature, they still put all their energy into creating new life. Squirrels, who have resorted to eating bitter spruce buds, are chasing each other in a frenzy to reproduce. Foxes and fishers, who might have

trouble breaking through crusty snow to access mice,
are traveling widely to defend their breeding territories.
Whitetail does and mothers of all kinds are nurturing their
unborn young with the last reserves of their own bodies.

I understand the warblers who return in the warmth
of spring to feast on our plentiful insects and raise
their young in the bounty of summer. It is harder to
comprehend the skunk who must rouse himself out of
his warm burrow in the early dawn of spring and traipse
across a frozen landscape with the intention of creating
new life. How can he even be sure that nature will
provide warmth and food again?

Animals have this faith built right into their genomes.
You might call it instinct or adaptation.

Plants who stored starches in their roots last fall,
carefully prepared buds many months before spring, and
crafted nutrient-filled seeds in the dog days of summer,
also have this faith.

Insects are waiting patiently, too. Long ago in the
shortening days of fall, they found a protected place to
hide. Some overwinter as adults, some as larvae or pupae,
and some as eggs. The individual may not survive, but the
cycle of life continues.

Underneath two feet of dense snow lies a carpet of
aspen leaves with little green islands where moth pupae
wait for spring. Inside goldenrod galls, the fly larvae have
not yet pupated and still risk death at the piercing beak of
a downy woodpecker.

Ticks will soon become active in widening patches of bare, sunny, forest floor.

Wood frogs, still frozen under the snow, are poised to thaw at the first chance. Spotted salamanders wait in their tunnels below the frost line. Their cells contain little bits of algae who are waiting to emerge into the sunlight and begin photosynthesis.

Loons are in their breeding plumage and have started moving north. They will fly to the edge of winter and make forays each day to check on the progression of ice-out. Turkey vultures have already arrived.

If you, too, feel that tunnel of gray ensnaring you, just look to the sky. The cycles of spring restore our faith in the power of life.

Furry Little Monsters

Reese Leann Gbur, age 10

The vivid blue sky was fading into a rainbow sherbet of color as the warm, spring sun sank toward the horizon. Crusty snow made for fast and challenging skiing, especially where the afternoon sun had shone strongest, resulting in a glaze of ice in the tracks. It took all of my balance to descend the steep hills safely.

On a gentle slope through a stand of spruce, the skiing suddenly wasn't so fast anymore. Hundreds of little spruce branch-tips littered the ground and, of course, seemed to congregate right in the ski tracks. Sticking and stumbling down the hill, I cursed the furry little monsters who ruined my glide.

Those furry monsters have been busy! Hemlock twigs littered the ground along the Forest Lodge Nature Trail where I had been snowshoeing earlier, and ski trails all over the area were sprinkled with green through every spruce and hemlock stand. I guess I can't be too mad at the furry mon . . . red squirrels. Spruce and hemlock buds are not their preferred food, but at this time of year with the supply of pine and spruce cones dwindling and acorns trapped under crusty snow, the squirrels still have to eat. So eat they do, by nipping off a branch tip, turning it around, nibbling off the bud, and throwing the rest right onto my ski trail.

Red squirrels are highly selective in their foraging behavior, harvesting cones from the tree species with the highest energy seeds first and systematically working their way through species of conifers by energy density per cone. As spring progresses and hunger gnaws, squirrels will also dine on poplar buds and catkins, elm buds, and maple buds. They will even drink a little sap from the maples once they have opened a wound. Mushrooms are another favorite food.

As the days lengthen, red squirrels begin to think amorous thoughts, and you may notice evidence of their "scramble competition" mating system. Males typically invade the territory of females in estrus and pursue them in vigorous mate chases. A single dominant male will pursue a female and drive off other subordinate males using calls or direct chase. Timing is essential, since she will only be receptive for a single afternoon. Keep your eyes and ears open for signs of this wild scramble in the woods.

Nesting sites are located within 100 feet of a cone cache. Red squirrels are highly territorial, with their food cache, called a midden, as the center of focus. Caches help female squirrels assess the resources available for reproduction and withstand years of low cone numbers. Red squirrels will vocally defend their territory with a full repertoire of rattles, screeches, growls, buzzes, and chirps. Because red squirrels often cache all their food in a single midden, they must defend it more fiercely than gray squirrels who have many smaller, dispersed food caches.

Not every cone in the cache will be eaten. Red squirrels use their excellent sense of smell to locate buried middens—even beneath four meters of snow! But the death of the owner or other circumstances can lead to middens being abandoned. When this happens, some of the seeds are left to germinate.

Planting seeds is not the only service squirrels provide to the forest. Fungi that help trees acquire nutrients are spread through caching as well. In addition, as squirrels nibble off the buds of conifers, it can cause the trees to grow multiple tops. While this is bad for the tree and timber value, it provides nest sites for a variety of birds and mammals and keeps forest diversity high.

While I might curse those furry little monsters for slowing my skis, I can still appreciate their important role in the forests I enjoy so much.

Desert Adaptations in the Northwoods?

Caroline Perkins

The thick blanket of fresh, white snow reflected bright rays up and under the brim of my cap. A vivid, blue sky stretched overhead as the intense spring sun rose above the twiggy treetops. Ski tracks that had been crunchy with ice just 30 minutes ago were now softening as the temperature rose steeply from a nighttime low of 18 degrees to a daytime high of 45. The one thorn in my day was an uncomfortable crack in the winter-dry skin of my left heel.

It was amazing to be skiing in late April in Wisconsin. This particular day, with its bluebird sky, bright sun, and warm temperatures, reminded me of another spring ski in a faraway land called Utah.

In 2005 I did an internship with the National Park Service leading school field trips and working in the visitor center in the Needles District of Canyonlands National Park. I lived in the tiny little town of Monticello (very similar to Cable!) at the base of the Abajo Mountains. Even though the word *abajo* means "low," the mountains tower above the intricately carved sandstone canyons of the park.

One weekend my roommate and I took our skis and drove up the mountain road to where the snowplows stopped. From there we skied over the snow-packed pass and stood breathless at the view. From the midst of winter, we looked out on a sunbaked, summer landscape of red rock canyons below fluffy, white clouds. The view fueled our anticipation for spring. The only thorn in my day was cracked lips from the desert-dry air.

It might not appear that Wisconsin and the Desert Southwest have much in common, but I found enough similarities in Utah to feel at home there, too. The snow, for one, was a nice connection. And half-buried in that snow were manzanita bushes with small, waxy, evergreen leaves on short woody stems. They bore a resemblance to their cousins, other plants in the Ericaceae family, who are some of my favorite residents of Wisconsin bogs.

In a bog there are quite a few plants with those small, waxy, evergreen leaves. Leatherleaf's name advertises its tough appendages, while the lovely names of bog rosemary, bog laurel, small cranberry, and snowberry contrast with their hardy leaves. All are in the Ericaceae family.

Down in the desert canyons, the fuzzy leaves of
sagebrush, Indian paintbrush, globe mallow, and the
in-rolled leaves of mountain mahogany also reminded me
of my Wisconsin home. That might seem odd, but have
you looked at the underside of a Labrador tea leaf from
your local bog lately? The leaf margins roll in on a dense
patch of woolly, orange hair, and hairs also carpet the
tightly curled leaves of its neighbor, bog rosemary.

Why might desert plants and bog plants have
characteristics in common? For one thing, they both deal
with a lack of water and the presence of desiccating winds
during part of the year. But aren't bogs soggy? Well, yes,
but not when they are frozen, a condition that can extend
late into spring. Plus, sometimes the peat in bogs builds
up so much that plants are elevated above the water table.
Deserts and bogs are also poor in nutrients due to slow
decomposition rates.

Evergreen leaves are great for contending with low
nutrient availability and short growing seasons. When
plants do not need to grow new leaves each year, they are
less dependent on nutrients getting recycled. However,
unlike deciduous leaves, evergreen leaves must deal with the
absence of liquid water in winter (or even year-round). The
thick, waxy cuticle is a plant's first defense, since it reduces
water loss from evaporation. It serves the same purpose as
the beeswax-based salve I massage into the cracked, dry
skin of my heel and lips. This protective wax is as useful in
Wisconsin winters as it is in the deserts of Utah!

Although waxy leaves help protect them from drying out, plants still need to exchange some gasses through their stomata to carry out photosynthesis. Stomata are pores in the leaf that allow gas exchange. Along with taking in the carbon dioxide necessary for photosynthesis, water vapor can also escape during transpiration. To reduce this loss, plants—both here and in the desert—create a "boundary layer."

The boundary layer is a thin zone of calm air hugging the surface of the leaf. In this layer the conditions are less harsh (less hot and dry) than in the wider world, and the temperature and moisture gradient is less steep. Therefore, the larger the boundary layer, the slower the rate of water loss. Hairy and in-rolled leaf margins increase the size of the boundary layer and slow water loss. Humans create their own boundary layers with fuzzy wool sweaters and fleecy mittens.

Standing on the edge of winter in Wisconsin and admiring the view of a distant spring may look quite different from southeast Utah, but similarities can be found across all communities if we are willing to take a closer look.

The Smell of Spring

Donna Post

Warm, midday sun had softened the snowpack, but a late afternoon chill refroze the drifts into a hard crust. I crunched loudly down my driveway on snowshoes, thinking about warm soup and a relaxing evening. As I neared the house, a familiar odor wafted toward me. Ah, the smell of Gusto, I thought. Gusto is a scent lure that trappers use as a "long distance call." According to the product description on the F&T Fur Harvester's Trading Post website, Gusto will entice red fox, gray fox, coyotes, bobcats, fishers, and martens to check out traps, which is why the pine marten researchers staying at the staff house used it on their hair snares for the past two months.

When I joined Phil and Caroline on a field day, the final step in resetting each hair snare was to squirt a generous amount of Gusto in a Dixie® cup on a tree above the trap. Did it attract martens? Phil would only discover the answer to that question when he analyzed the DNA of the hair samples and sorted out the martens from the weasels and other nontarget species who may have investigated the traps as well.

Whether or not Gusto aided Phil's research, it left a strong impression on *us*. According to the Gusto sales pitch: "When you crack the cap, you will certainly smell skunk, but underneath you will detect a sweet odor consisting of a generous dose of castor and muskrat musk. To top it off, Gusto contains 'special agents' and it is put up in a thick base, so it hangs in there for a long time." And boy does it! I could often smell the pungent odor from the end of our long driveway. On warm days, especially, it seemed to radiate from the researchers' work truck. It wasn't entirely unpleasant, but definitely unusual.

But Phil and Caroline had moved out a couple days ago now, and to have the scent of Gusto linger that long seemed a little extreme. Back at the house, I took off my snowshoes and headed toward the front door. The smell intensified, which was unusual since I was walking away from where the truck had parked. I paused for a moment to contemplate this.

Then I glanced down at a cardboard box on the patio, rakishly tipped on its side. It held a very fluffy, black tail with white highlights along the outer edges. Of course! It was an actual skunk that made my driveway smell like skunk.

The stark white and black coloration of skunks is not necessarily camouflage for their nocturnal endeavors. Instead, its function is to warn potential predators of the skunk's distastefulness. Similarly, the bright orange color of a monarch butterfly warns birds of its toxicity.

The books all say that when a skunk is threatened, it first tries to run away from the predator. Well, this skunk just buried its head deeper inside the box. ("If I can't see you, you can't see me!") Luckily for me, striped skunks usually do not discharge the foul-smelling contents of their scent glands unless mortally threatened. When faced with danger, a skunk turns away from the predator with an arched back and erect tail. It may also stomp its feet.

When they are mortally threatened, skunks bend into a U-shape with both head and rump facing the enemy. They then emit two streams of fluid from scent glands located just inside the anus, which meet after traveling about a foot, finally spreading into a fine mist that can travel up to 15 feet.

This defense works pretty well against mammals with a well-developed sense of smell, so skunks are rarely preyed upon by foxes, wolves, or badgers. Large birds are not bothered, though, and great horned owls are skunks' main predators.

Though they do not support a diversity of predators, skunks themselves enjoy a wide variety of prey. Insects compose about 70 percent of their diet, and skunks are one of the main predators of bees. When attacking a beehive, they wait for the angry bees to emerge from the hive, then bat them out of the air and eat them.

Since bees and other insects, earthworms, snails, frogs, bird eggs, berries, and nuts are all in short supply in early spring, it is a little surprising that skunks are even awake. But skunks aren't true hibernators in the first place, and I've seen skunk tracks (probably from a restless male) even during a January thaw. These days, chickadees, great horned owls, and eagles aren't the only ones getting a little amorous. Skunks mate from mid-February to mid-April and naturally become more active during this time.

A skunk's four to eight babies will be born in May or June. They are hairless, but somehow already have their striping pattern. Although it takes 22 days for their eyes to open, the little tykes can supposedly spray their musk after just eight days. It seems fitting that an animal who scientists call *Mephitis mephitis,* which means "a poisonous or foul-smelling gas emitted from the earth," would live up to its name right from birth. Ah, the smell of spring!

Not Necessarily Pretty

Victoria Zalatoris

The warm wind smells fresh and damp and brings with it sunshine, birdsong, and melting snow.

In places, though, the breeze carries an unpleasant scent, sometimes described as a mixture of burning truck tires, decaying meat, and garlic. If you follow your nose upwind, you may find yourself in a mostly frozen swamp. Black ash

and red maple trees stand like skeletons against the sky.
Dogwood and alder shrubs form thickets around the edges.

If you are brave enough to explore on the rotten ice,
you may find something rotten indeed—or at least
something trying to make you think it's rotten! This is the
home of the skunk cabbage.

They are more conspicuous in summer when their
large, green leaves grow in tall rosettes, but they are more
interesting in spring. The blossoms of skunk cabbage
deliberately smell like dead stuff to attract early spring
pollinators like carrion beetles.

The insects not only get a snack when they visit a
skunk cabbage; they also get a warm place to rest. Skunk
cabbages are able to bloom so early because they produce
heat and melt their way up through the ice. The heat is
released through the oxidation and breakdown of sugars,
an essential process in human metabolism as well.

During the two weeks when skunk cabbages flower,
they consume about the same amount of oxygen as a small
mammal of comparable size. In fact, one researcher has
quipped that they are "more skunk than cabbage." This
high metabolism allows the plant to regulate itself like a
warm-blooded animal, maintaining a temperature of about
30 degrees above the outside air.

To accomplish this energetically costly feat, skunk
cabbages prepared the previous summer by storing lots of
starch in their roots. They also pre-formed their flower bud,
which overwintered as a tightly closed bundle just a few
inches tall.

The purple and yellow apostrophe-shaped flowers are not necessarily pretty, but then, not much is this time of year. The woods are drab and wet.

With more sunshine and warm days, that will change quickly. The drab, stinky skunk cabbage will be replaced by vibrant yellow marsh marigolds, delicate purple hepatica, and the sweet smell of honeysuckle on the breeze.

The Breeze of Balance

Laura Semken

A fresh breeze sighs loudly through the tops of the pine trees and gently stirs the air on the forest floor . . . A warm breath of spring, tiptoeing in from the south, brings the scent of warm soil and wet leaves . . . A gale from the north swoops over my shoulder and sends ripples racing across the sparkling surface of Lake Superior.

The month of March is known for being windy. In a slow spring, April can be just as blustery. Sometimes it wears on me—the constant battle, the whipping hair, and the unceasing noise—but some days it's invigorating and refreshing.

In some cultures wind is a symbol of unity, freedom, eternity, and balance. It is as true ecologically as it is metaphorically.

The first time I encountered wind as a symbol of unity, I was on the south shore of Lake Superior at a wedding on a piney point. A stiff breeze whipped through the trees and blew out the unity candle. With great aplomb the minister launched into a beautiful and extemporaneous sermon on wind as a symbol of unity. As the air swirled around the guests and the happy couple, we imagined how all of our breaths came from and returned to the one body of air that surrounded us and the entire globe.

In some cultures wind is personified as a divine messenger who is able to manipulate unseen energy. Indeed, wind is the main method our Earth uses to equal out differences in temperature. Energy from the Sun warms the earth and the air above it, but it does not heat everything evenly. As warm air rises, cool air flows in to replace it.

The stronger the difference in temperature, the stronger the winds created. Think of it this way: In summer the temperature difference between northern Wisconsin and southern Florida is not that great. Winds are relatively calm. In the winter, however, the temperature difference increases. In order for our atmosphere to remain in equilibrium, the winds mixing warmer and colder air must speed up. Wind is the Earth's attempt to find a temperature balance.

Wind disperses more than just heat. When strong winds carry away dirt, microbes in the soil become hitchhikers along for the ride. Nutrients and organisms lost from one region may be deposited across the globe. Organisms may colonize otherwise inaccessible regions. Nutrients blown around the globe help forested areas obtain trace amounts of minerals. Some organisms get a significant amount of nutrients from dust on the wind. Lichens and epiphytes ("air plants") are two examples.

Insects also use the wind for long-distance travel. How high can they fly? Researchers calculated that "on any given day, the air column rising 50–15,000 feet above one square mile of Louisiana countryside contained an average of 25 million insects"[1] (from my current bedside book, *Insectopedia* by Hugh Raffles). At the upper limit—15,000 feet—there was a ballooning spider who used her silk as a kite. Butterflies, dragonflies, gnats, water striders, leaf bugs, booklice, and katydids have been sighted hundreds of miles out on the open ocean, and aphids have been found on ice floes. Some wingless insects (and plankton!) are plucked from their earthly tethers by a sharp gust of wind, but few are completely passive travelers.

Wind also helps lakes balance their nutrients and

chemicals throughout various layers during fall and spring turnover. In the fall when the surface water cools to about the same temperature as the lower water, the wind can mix the water masses together (fall turnover) and even out the temperature and oxygen levels. A similar process occurs during spring turnover. As ice melts and colder surface waters warm to the temperature of bottom waters, the lake mixes. Water from the lake bottom brings nutrients up with it.

With every breath we invite the universe in. As the spring winds swirl around you, take a moment to appreciate the wind's role in encouraging balance and unity in our sometimes stormy world.

Maple Syrup

Mason McKay, age 10

The amber-colored liquid glowed warmly from inside the Mason jar. "Isn't it beautiful!" crowed Deb, the proud owner of this jewel-colored treasure and a brand-new participant in the age-old tradition of tapping maple trees for syrup. We all agreed it was lovely and licked our spoons thoroughly after the taste test.

Maple sap carries sugars, water, and other nutrients up from the tree trunk and roots, where it was stored for the winter, and into the twigs and buds where the solution fuels new growth in the spring. Since sap only runs profusely before the leaves emerge and when temperatures fluctuate between warm, sunny days and below-freezing nights, sugaring season is relatively brief. Innovative humans figured out how to tap into this wonderful resource, and that practice continues on both small and industrial scales today.

Humans aren't the only creatures who know the secrets of the maple tree, though. An Iroquois legend explains that Native Americans initially learned how to collect sap from maple trees by watching red squirrels cutting into tree bark with their teeth and later returning to lick the sap. Acclaimed naturalist, Bernd Heinrich, author of *Winter World* and *Summer World* (two of my favorite books), was the first to describe this behavior for science.

Heinrich watched as red squirrels near his cabin in Maine used their teeth to make a "single pair of chisel-like grooves that punctured the tree to the sap-bearing xylem."[2] Most impressive to me is that the squirrels didn't try to drink the dilute sap immediately. Instead, they gave the water in the sap some time to evaporate and came back early the next morning—before the sap started running again—to enjoy the more concentrated syrup.

Not only do red squirrels have their own evaporating method, they also choose carefully when to tap the trees.

Squirrels know that any time the leaves are off and the temperatures are fluctuating, sap will flow. They are able to tap the trees when the conditions are right in the fall and winter, as well as early spring.

Yellow-bellied sapsuckers are woodpeckers who also tap maple trees in the early spring. During the spring syruping season, they need only to make a narrow, circular hole in the bark to get the sugar they crave.

During the summer months, sap doesn't flow through the xylem in the same way, but sugar manufactured in the leaves is being transported through the phloem. Phloem sap may contain 20–30 percent sugar, far higher than the 2–3 percent sugar in xylem sap.

Sapsuckers are the experts in summer sap tapping. They drill shallow, quarter-inch, rectangular sap wells in a variety of tree species and use their brush-like tongues to lap up the sap that accumulates. Once the tree scars over the hole and the flow subsides, the birds drill another row of holes above the first. The pattern of holes sapsuckers use may force more sap through their newest holes as some vessels are constricted and sap flow is diverted. But sugar isn't their only goal. Sapsuckers also eat the nutritious inner bark as they chisel and nab insects who come to steal the sugar.

Sapsuckers are one of our earliest returning migrants, and only about three weeks behind them come male hummingbirds intent on claiming a nesting territory. Not many flowers are blooming when the hummingbirds arrive, so the tiny birds take advantage of nectar-like sap from sapsucker wells. In return, they chase off some of the 30 plus other species of birds who may steal the sap.

The sap from sapsucker wells also nourishes a host of other animals, including squirrels, bats, porcupines, and insects from at least 20 different families, such as bees, wasps, hornets, and moths. Snow fleas, who look like flakes of black pepper on the snow, sometimes become pests in sap buckets.

Michael J. Caduto emphasizes the importance of sapsuckers to our northern forest communities in an article published in *Northern Woodlands* magazine: "Studies show that the diversity of many forest species, as well as the size of the population of each species, is greater in areas with high levels of sapsucker activity. Because of this effect, sapsuckers are considered a keystone species— they have a critical impact on the surrounding ecological community that goes beyond what would normally be expected from their numbers."[3]

The amber-colored maple syrup in the Mason jar must be special. It not only has the ability to connect Deb with her friends, her woods, and an ancient tradition, but it also connects dozens of species in fascinating and important relationships that make our community stronger.

And, it tastes great on pancakes!

Change

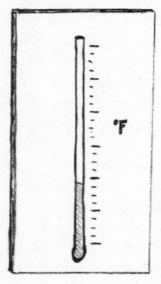

Alyssa Core

I've been mulling some things over for a few months now.
First it was instinct and faith. Spring is a time of rebirth
and renewal for almost everything, and organisms follow
age-old clues to schedule their spring events. As we all
wait for the relative ease of summer, looking to the sky can
be a comfort no matter what you believe is up there.

Then I got philosophical about wind and how it's both
a symbol and a source of unity, freedom, eternity, and
balance. Most importantly for this time of year, the wind is
the Earth's attempt to find a temperature balance.

Finally I shared stories of the many amazing organisms

(including humans!) that look forward to the maple sap run each year.

While I was writing, something else was gnawing at my brain: an unpleasant, but fascinating understanding of how these three topics, and many others, are connected to each other, and to our actions.

In 2012 University of Wisconsin-Madison professor Steve Vavrus and a colleague at Rutgers University published a paper hypothesizing that warming in the Arctic would cause the jet stream to slow down and meander like a river flowing through the Great Plains. This, in turn, transports less warm air from the oceans over the land and sets the stage for more extreme weather.[4]

The big-picture mechanism for this connection between warm oceans and slow-moving/extreme weather isn't hard to understand. Wind moves from high pressure to low pressure and equalizes temperature differences. When the temperatures aren't as different, the wind doesn't have as much oomph. Melting ice in the Arctic, Vavrus explained, allows heat stored in the ocean to escape to the atmosphere where it changes the pressure patterns.

It came as no surprise to the scientists then, when record-low sea ice coverage in the Arctic during the summer of 2012 was followed by the coldest March in Wisconsin in 3,540 years, and a cold April full of slow-moving blizzards. Professor Vavrus acknowledged that there's some natural fluctuation of the circulation patterns, and that weather and climate are different things. He told

Wisconsin Public Radio, "We're arguing the loss of sea ice is . . . loading the dice in favor of a more negative Arctic oscillation pattern."[5] It's loading the dice for extreme, unusual, and sometimes unpleasant weather.

The same meandering jet stream, Vavrus noted, could also explain unusually warm springs. If a meandering jet stream is like a river, some bends are favorable to cold spells; others are favorable to extreme warmth. Either way, these unusual weather patterns are symptoms of climate change.

While we might be frustrated by the deep and persistent snow during one spring, people preparing to tap maple trees would be just as disappointed by an early heat wave that severely shortens sugaring season. Cold nights are necessary for strong sap flow, and early bud-break stops it.

As temperatures fluctuate from warm enough to cold again, the sap starts and then stops flowing. High winds steal away heat that trees absorb from the sun, slowing sap flow. Some sugarbushes report record sap flow, while others haven't even begun.

Wisconsin is one of the highest sap-producing states, and the crop value of syrup can be more than $5.8 million a year. The value of this ancient tradition in terms of cultural history is immeasurable. (Read more at www.climatewisconsin.org.)

Maple trees use temperature to cue their sap flow, but other organisms rely on day length and sunlight intensity to prompt spring events. Many creatures in each category rely on each other for food, pollination, or other symbiotic services. What happens, then, when the day length and the temperature do not match up like the creatures expect? Will their faith in the progress of spring serve them well? Or will old instincts and adaptations not work in a changing climate?

These are heavy questions to ponder, as I trudge through the slush with sleet pelting my face. The balance brought by wind, the comfort of the sky, the renewal of spring . . . will these change, too?

Leaf It to Me, Buddy!

Brooke Sapper, age 16

While we celebrate fall colors in Wisconsin and elsewhere for their variety and vibrancy, spring colors will also impress the attentive observer. After the snow melts and we enter another round of "stick season," the drab woods can be a little discouraging. Grass and weeds green up first, since many of them are immigrants from the Russian steppe. To survive in that cold grassland, the plants have adapted to breaking dormancy at much lower temperatures than our locals.

Many leafy things that are green now—Tartarian

honeysuckle, common speedwell, lilacs, and dandelions—
are not native here. The few evergreen natives, like
wintergreen, partridge berry, clubmoss, and pipsissewa,
have thick, waxy leaves to protect from them frost and
desiccation.

If we are patient, color rises slowly in the trees, and
soon the forests are washed with the soft greens and pinks
of bursting buds and fresh new leaves. Those buds formed
months ago, during the steamy days of summer. The plant
organized the basic cells for shoots, leaves, and flowers,
and encased them in protective scales or dense hairs.

All winter, tiny and important, they waited for the right
cue. Some did not survive. Grouse, purple finches, deer,
squirrels, moose, rabbits, and hares all know what a fine
winter food source those little bundles are. Bright red
basswood buds are sweet enough for me to nibble, too.

But what's the right cue? Naturalists have pondered
this for many years. We struggle to design experiments
that can control all the variables and provide answers that
we can generalize across species and locations. The best
explanation is that budbreak is determined by a complex
interplay of factors involving genetics, day length, cold
exposure, and warmth.

Once budbreak happens, there are still more mysteries
to ponder. Ever since I can remember, miniature spring
leaves have fascinated me. Oak leaves, in particular, start
out wonderfully red and fuzzy, with all their little lobes and
wrinkly veins. The rich color is a result of anthocyanin, the

same pigment that protects leaves in the fall. Before a leaf
has filled with chlorophyll, excess sunlight can be damaging.
Anthocyanin acts as a sunscreen and antioxidant. The fuzz
protects tender young leaves from frost the same way a
wool sweater keeps you warm—by trapping warmer air next
to the surface.

Leaf growth is another natural mystery. A combination
of cell number, cell size, and intercellular space determines
a leaf's size. Leaf cells within the bud are preprogramed to
grow with a certain pattern, and emerging leaves use the
plant's built-in orientation system to determine their axis
of growth.

Just like scientists have developed a computer model to
simulate birds and fish moving in flocks or schools, they
have created a computer model that uses simple rules of
leaf growth to grow an accurate "virtual" leaf.

Cells at the leaf margins and on the leaf's surface layer
are especially important in determining leaf and petal
size. They're genetically programmed to secrete growth
hormones that encourage leaf cells to divide. As the cells
expand, the hormones inside are diluted and growth
stops. Animals use this same principal of dilution
(although with different hormones) to determine
size (like on the wings of a fly, for example). Uneven
cell growth results in leaves and flowers with the
characteristic sizes and shapes that we recognize.

Once leaves mature, they begin to photosynthesize.
Energy is transferred from photons of sunlight to

chlorophyll molecules and into a complex photosystem. Then plants can break apart molecules of carbon dioxide and water and recombine them into sugars. From simple sugars, they make carbohydrates and cellulose, and with those building blocks, they begin the process of forming a new palette of buds for next spring.

Little Solar Panels

Miya McKay, age 7

As the days get longer and the trees leaf out, spring ephemeral wildflowers race to soak in as much sunshine as possible. Spring beauties, wild leeks (ramps), Dutchman's breeches, wood anemone, bloodroot, and trout lily are some of the most beautiful treasures of spring. They rush out of the ground each year, sometimes while snow still haunts the north-facing slopes. Flowers bloom, leaves unfurl, bees hum, ants crawl, seeds set, photosynthesis produces sugars, starch is stored back into the roots, and then—just as the tree leaves above are reaching their full potential—the flowers' ephemeral leaves melt back into the duff.

Spring ephemeral wildflowers have figured out that they can make use of the rich soil in the shady depths of deciduous forests, as long as they can get a head start on the trees. Partly because they only appear for such a short time each spring, they have captured many a heart. They also capture many a photon.

Photons are little packets of energy that travel through space. We know them as light. They carry energy from the Sun (released during nuclear fusion reactions) to the Earth. Once here, they provide almost all the energy for life on Earth. Plants, like these lovely spring ephemerals, are an essential link between the Sun and animals, since we animals cannot capture sunlight on our own.

For a few short weeks in spring, the flowers mentioned above absorb photons like crazy. Through the process of photosynthesis, plants use the photons' energy to split carbon dioxide from the air and water from the soil, and recombine those molecules into sugar.

During one May, I explored the process of photosynthesis with first graders who came to the Museum for field trips. We acted out a food chain starting with the Sun, and then shrank down so we could be magically transported into a leaf. There we met Chef Chlorophyll, the green pigment that mixes the ingredients of photosynthesis. The students raced around the yard, gathering sunlight (yellow water), water (blue water), and air (drinking straws) to create a frothy green soup in the mixing bowl. Finally we each ate a grape, and considered how plants produce the sugars we eat every day in a cornucopia of different forms.

The sugars produced by spring ephemerals are not distributed in sweet fruits, though. These plants mostly produce hard, dry seeds without a grape's juicy cradle of flesh. Instead, their precious sugars are stored as carbohydrates (complex sugars) in starchy roots. Burrow your finger into the soft soil near any of these plants, and you will soon pull out a small, white tuber. The tubers of trout lilies and spring beauties have a mildly sweet flavor. Leek tubers store their sugar with an oniony kick. Dutchman's breeches and bloodroots store their sugar with toxins added.

Spring ephemerals use the energy stored in these tubers to get a head start on the tree leaves each spring, and then rush to replenish their pantries for next year.

All summer long, other plants will be capturing the energy from photons of sunlight and storing it in their roots, stems, leaves, flowers, fruits, and seeds. Humans harness that energy in a myriad of ways. Think about that as you eat your dinner salad, turn on the television, plant your garden, drive your car, and drink your morning coffee! Energy from the Sun is integral to every aspect of our lives.

Little Packets of Fatty Goodness

Mason McKay, age 10

After you notice one, you see them everywhere. Despite the chilly breeze and gray skies, my eyes never stopped scanning the dry, brown leaf litter as the group hiked the trail to St. Peter's Dome. When I noticed the first tightly furled spike of trillium leaves that had worked its way up through the dry maple leaves, we stopped to search for more.

As our eyes adjusted, our mental search images honed, and the tiny, green spikes appeared everywhere. Although we could not identify the spikes, we knew from last year that these could be wood anemone, large-flowered trillium, violets, Dutchman's breeches, and bloodroot.

The fully unfurled leaves of spring beauty, barely over an inch long, clustered in the shelter of a fallen log.

Many of these spring flowers have a symbiotic relationship with ants. In a month or so when they have finished blooming and have gone to seed, a soap opera emerges. All the wildflowers I listed above attach a packet of fatty goodness—like a donut for ants—to the outsides of their seeds. Called an elaiosome, this little morsel of energy-rich lipids, amino acids, and other nutrients shows that the way into an ant's hill is through its stomach.

Ants carry the elaiosome, still attached to its seed, into their hill. There the ants may feed it to their larvae or eat it themselves. The seed, which is smooth, hard, tough to hold on to, and impossible to eat, is thrown into the ants' midden or garbage heap. Here, in a nitrogen- and phosphorus-rich environment, among moist, decaying plant matter and the bodies of dead ants, the seed has a wonderful place to grow. It is safe from birds, other insects, and even forest fires. This type of ant-assisted seed dispersal is called myrmecochory.

Myrmecochory (mur–me-co-cory) is exhibited by more than 3,000 plant species worldwide and is present in every major biome on all continents except Antarctica. One study determined that it has evolved at least 100 separate times in 55 different plant families.

In nature, when there is success, there is often a cheater. Hepatica, a beautiful purple or white spring flower that emerges before its leaves, is an unassuming swindler.

Instead of providing a detachable treat for the ant, hepatica covers its seeds in nonremovable elaiosomes with the same chemical cues as its neighbors' true elaiosomes.

When ants take hepatica's seeds back to the nest, the elaiosome can't be eaten, and the chemical cues stay intact. Instead of being stripped of its packet of fatty goodness and thrown into the trash heap, the hepatica seed stimulates each ant who passes by to pick it up by the permanent, fatty handle and carry it somewhere else. Hepatica saves energy by not making a large elaiosome, and it benefits when its seeds are distributed more widely. In return for their dispersal services, the ants get nothing. Hepatica is a parasite!

If cheaters win, though, then pretty soon everyone starts cheating. For a mutualism (a symbiotic relationship where both parties benefit) to continue, it must provide appropriate rewards. Scientists have found that seeds with tasty, edible, true elaiosomes are transported by ants much more often than the cheater seeds of hepatica and others like it. "In this situation, cheating . . . establishes a background against which better mutualists can display competitive superiority, thus leading . . . to the reinforcement of the mutualism,"[6] reports Ferriere in the Proceedings of the Royal Society of London.

Such drama, on what may seem like a small scale, impacts entire ecosystems on six continents. In this northern hardwood forest, maple leaves cushioned my knees as I crouched down to look closer at the just-opened flowers of Dutchman's breeches. A bit of movement caught the corner of my eye, and I shifted my focus to a patch of soft moss. A tiny, black ant was scrambling its way across a jungle of leaves. As my gaze widened, I noticed another ant, and then another, and another, all busy with their own lives. After you notice one, you see them everywhere.

Salamanders and the Sun

Marlene Ehresman

I love spring. It is invigorating to watch everything wake up and start growing.

I can't imagine that I will ever stop being amazed by living things who can take carbon dioxide from the air, water from the soil, energy from the Sun, and make sugar. This time of year it seems like everything is doing it: pine trees, lilac bushes, evergreen woodferns, spring beauties, algae, and salamanders. Yes, salamanders.

Vernal pools are a spring phenomenon. Puddles of snowmelt and spring rains form in low areas, and may last a few days or a few months. The key is that they dry up eventually, which makes them poor habitat for fish. Amphibians, like frogs and salamanders, take advantage of this lack of predators and lay their eggs in the relatively safe, warm water. Their young feed on mosquito larvae and other insects who also use the pools to breed.

One vernal pool, near the old quarry at St. Peter's Dome, has several jelly-covered clusters of spotted salamander eggs. Spotted salamanders are common throughout the eastern United States. Their large size, blue-black skin, and bright-yellow spots make them charismatic critters. Adults mostly live in moist leaf litter and under rotting logs. In the spring they journey by the hundreds to vernal pools to mate and lay eggs.

The jelly around the eggs keeps them from drying out, but it also inhibits oxygen diffusion into the egg. Scientists have known for a while that the salamanders have a symbiotic relationship with algae to help address this issue. Algae on the jelly use the carbon dioxide and nitrogen-rich waste emitted by the developing embryo. In return, the photosynthesizing algae give off oxygen that the salamander embryo can use. The algae form a natural oxygen mask!

Recently, scientists discovered that spotted salamanders have an even closer relationship with algae. These algae are, in fact, located *inside* cells all over the spotted salamander's body. There are even signs that algae may be directly providing oxygen and sugars to the salamander cells that encapsulate them. Using an electron microscope, researchers viewed salamander mitochondria (the powerhouses of cells) gathering around algae like it was the dining room table. This is the first ever documentation of photosynthetic algae inside the cells of a vertebrate animal.[7]

Somehow salamanders have convinced their immune systems not to kill these foreign cells. Scientists think that salamanders' ability to regrow their limbs may have something to do with their ability to host foreign algae cells within their bodies. Scientists even found algae in the oviducts of adult female spotted salamanders, suggesting that mothers can pass the algae to their offspring.[7]

Salamanders. Algae. Amazing.

Fee-Bee

Diana Randolph

What are the signs of spring that you watch for each year? Birds returning, flowers blooming, insects hatching, frogs calling, and chipmunks scurrying—these are all milestones on the way to a brief Northwoods summer of warmth and sun.

One of my favorite early birds is the eastern phoebe. These dusky, brown flycatchers spend the winter in the southern United States or Mexico, and they are one of the earliest feathered friends to return each spring. They have learned to tolerate a human-altered landscape quite well, and often build their moss-and-mud nests on bridges, barns, and homes.

The first time I noticed a phoebe as a beginning birder I was completely baffled. They do not have striking markings. They do not stand out in the bird book. As I've become a better birder, I've realized that it's their call and their behavior—not their looks—that are helpfully distinctive.

Phoebes often perch low in trees or on fence lines, where their plump bodies and large, flat-topped heads are visible in silhouette. They frequently wag their tails down and up as they watch for flying insects. Then, *ZIP!* They dart out to catch the bug and often return to the same perch.

Many flycatchers share phoebes' shape and behavior. In northern Wisconsin we have about eight species of flycatchers, including great-crested and willow flycatchers, eastern kingbirds, and wood-pewees. Some flycatchers look so similar to each other that voice is the primary field mark. However, none of them (except the phoebe), commonly nest on your porch!

Phoebes are helpful to folks who are learning to bird by ear because they say their own name. The song is a raspy, two-parted "fee-bee," or a variation on that with a stutter in the second half. Like most birds, males are more vocal than females.

Other songbirds will spend one short period of brain development memorizing songs of adults and the next phase trying to match them. If a songbird does not grow up with adults of its own species, or is deaf, it does not develop a normal song. Phoebes don't need to do either! They don't need to hear other adults in order to produce the typical phoebe song, and they do not need to hear themselves sing to know that they are pronouncing their name correctly.

With my neighborhood phoebes calling cheerfully, darting out to catch insects, and building a nest, today feels like a great start to spring.

Murmuring Trees

Trees, trees, murmuring trees.

Black-throated Green Warbler

Rosemary Mosco, birdandmoon.com

"Trees, trees, murmuring trees!" Through closed windows
on a chilly morning, I hear the welcome song of an old
friend. It's followed by an emphatic chant from deeper in
the forest: "Teacher. Teacher! TEACHER. TEACHER!"
And then a buzzy, upward-trending "Parrrrrrrrula." I
catch a flash of movement out of the corner of my eye

49

and hear the squeaky "wee-see-wee-see-wee-see" of yet
another neighbor.

The warblers are back! Warblers are a group of active
little birds who are often colorful, insectivorous, and
(as their name suggests) vocal. They spend the winter
in exotic locales to the south and travel thousands of
miles on their tiny wings just to raise their young in the
Northwoods. You may be wondering what attracts them
all the way here from sunny Mexico and Costa Rica. Are
you reading this outside? Then the answer may be sucking
your blood or buzzing in your ear at this very moment.

Black flies. Mosquitoes. Gnats. The warblers come here
for the feast. Moths, wasps, bees, caterpillars, larvae of all
kinds, leaf beetles, bark beetles, weevils, ants, aphids (and
their honeydew), caddisflies, craneflies, mayflies, stoneflies,
dragonflies, grasshoppers, and locusts. During outbreaks
of pests like the spruce budworm, warblers become
rainbow-colored exterminators.

Could we please have a resounding "Thank You!" for
the warblers? Let us put them on a pedestal with spiders
and bats and thank them all for eating insects.

Not only do warblers control pests, they also look and
sound delightful while doing it. For those of you who
are curious, the bird songs mentioned in the opening
scene belong to black-throated green warblers, ovenbirds,
northern parulas, and black-and-white warblers.

A Little Bit of Good in Every Bad

Mollie Kreb

The peas are planted, the beans are watered, tomatoes are towering, and the basil is thriving. Gardening season is in full swing, which means that I'm feeling happier and smarter than I have all winter. This is not just an anecdotal "I love gardening" testimonial—there is scientific research to support my claim.

During those long, hot hours I spend toiling in the dirt, my body is synthesizing vitamin D. This fat-soluble compound is linked to depression prevention, immune system strength, bone health, and more. I can't quite do photosynthesis like my tomatoes, but at least I can make something useful from sunlight!

It is not just the sunshine that makes gardeners so happy this time of year; it is also the fresh air. We inhale an elixir of happiness from the soil. A common soil bacteria—*Mycobacterium vaccae*—has been shown to increase serotonin (a happy chemical in your brain) levels in mice. Not only does this decrease anxiety, it also makes the mice smarter!

Mice given the bacteria navigated a maze twice as fast as control mice. The effects do not last long, though, and scientists surmise that humans would need to be exposed about once a week in order to reap the benefits of these healthy bacteria.

Unfortunately, gardening season coincides with another season as well. Everywhere that clean, fast-flowing streams laugh and tumble down rocky paths, tiny larvae cling to the submerged surfaces of rocks and logs. At the business end of the tiny, worm-like creature is a pair of foldable fans. These fans strain passing debris from the fast-flowing water, and the larva scrapes a snack into its mouth every few seconds.

After seven to ten days of eating and growing, this little larva will pupate (like a butterfly spinning a chrysalis). The creature spends a week in the pupa, completely rearranging its body and developing the tools for a new way of life. Then, in a bubble of air, an adult black fly rises to the surface.

If it's a male black fly, we can pretty much ignore it. Males eat a little nectar, fertilize a female in flight, and die. Females may also use the sugary liquid to fuel their flight, but making eggs requires a blood meal. This is where gardeners, paddlers, hikers, anglers, and other outdoor enthusiasts come in. The black fly female will slash a little cut in your skin, inject an anticoagulant with her saliva, and drink her fill. No matter that her "fill" is approximately 0.00006 ounces; the bite's ill effects loom much larger. We end up with bleeding, itchy, swollen welts around wrists, beltlines, necklines, hairlines, and ankles.

Nothing in nature is all bad, though. These tiny tormentors feed tasty trout, beautiful birds, dashing dragonflies, and swooping swallows. Folklore claims that black flies pollinate blueberry flowers and improve fruit set, but the scientific jury is still out on that one.

In Maine the Black Fly Breeder's Association sells humorous T-shirts and donates the money to charity. One T-shirt design lauds black flies as "Defenders of the Wilderness," due to their ability to keep timid tourists at bay.

Despite the good qualities of black flies, we would all prefer to avoid them. Happily, they do not sneak indoors like mosquitoes, but indoors is not where the vitamin D and happy soil bacteria live. Dark-colored clothing, carbon dioxide, and perfumes all attract them. So it follows that if we would like to deter black flies, we should wear white, not exhale, and not wash our hair or use deodorant. As a side effect, many friends and colleagues would avoid us, too.

After five or six hot days, the tender little bodies of black flies (one sixth of an inch long!) dry out and black fly season is over.

Later in the summer, as my tomatoes ripen and the pea pods swell, I will be able to enjoy the sunshine and soil bacteria in an enlightened state of peace and happiness . . . interrupted only by the painful bite of horse flies.

A Delight for the Senses

Drew Guttormson

Springtime is a delight for the senses. Each morning when I venture outside, countless little pleasures tickle me awake. Pouring in through every portal come sounds, smells, sights, touches, and tastes of the season.

First, and long before the sun even thinks about rising, come the loon calls. The territorial pair in the bay near my house defends their space with maniacal yodels and distressed tremolos. As the horizon lightens to a soft pink, a hummingbird buzzes up to the feeder, the vireo starts to slur its morning greeting of "Here I am . . . Over here . . . In the trees . . . Where are you?" and the ovenbird shouts its "teacher Teacher TEACHER!" much too loudly for the early hour.

As I ride my bike along the county highway, birds singing in the swamps, fields, forests, and yards form a sort of sonic gauntlet. Trills, chatters, chips, warbles, whistles, and the downward spiraling, eerily flute-like calls of the veery fill my ears from every angle. In some wetlands the spring peepers still peep loudly. Geese honk, crows caw, and even the wind has a particular sound as it meanders through the emerging leaves. What have you been listening to?

On my ride home in the heat of the afternoon, sunbeams shine hot on every surface and release all of sorts of early summer smells. First there is the sweet smell of the apple tree on the edge of town, its snowy white flowers just humming with bees. Then there is the sulfurous smell of the swampy ditches, where plants, decomposing without oxygen all winter, have released their particular boggy perfume.

Warm trees have their own smell, as does the river as it rushes over the dam. The spray has a particular musty odor that I love. Then there is the funk of the deer repellent I spray on my cold frame garden because the vigorous broccoli plants can no longer fit under the glass. Soon the lilacs will bloom and release their enchanting perfume. What is your favorite spring smell?

The visual beauty of spring is almost too much to describe. Like many of you, I could fawn over each individual flower, the beautiful patchwork of greens in the developing leaves, or the reflections on a glass-calm lake.

To glimpse the neon-bright plumage of a scarlet tanager is a special treat. "The scarlet tanager flies through the green foliage as if it would ignite the leaves. You can hardly believe that a living creature can wear such colors,"[8] wrote naturalist Henry David Thoreau. Yet believe I must, since twice recently these blindingly gorgeous birds have darted across the road as I passed. Other folks—more than usual it seems—have reported seeing scarlet tanagers at their bird feeders, in their yards, and deep in the woods on birding walks. Where do your eyes feast these days?

As visual creatures we are biased toward looking at the world. Don't forget the pleasure of touch. Just this morning I paused to rub a baby hazel leaf between my fingers and was delighted by the delicate furriness of its crinkly surface. Even while focused on seeing a bird or a plant, our skin is at work, experiencing the world. Not even a scarlet tanager will distract me when I feel that particular tickle of a tick on my neck. Have you felt it, too?

Finally, for me, the taste of spring comes from the wild leeks who form a living carpet in the woods. Just walking through a patch fills the air with their pungent aroma. Not quite onions, not quite garlic—a wild scent all their own. One bite of a leaf will leave you with leek-breath for hours, but I still gather handfuls for my morning omelets and blend bunches into creamy pesto. What have you been nibbling on in the woods?

Have you been using your senses fully? Springtime is a perfect time to start!

The Smell of Rain

Ayla Baussan, age 6

Throughout the morning, the fluffy, white clouds grew larger and more numerous, cluttering the blue sky. The temperature on the bank sign rose sharply from 40 degrees in early morning to 77 degrees by early afternoon.

After lunch I stepped outside to run errands. A blast of hot, humid air met me at the door. We recently finished winter with a blizzard, and now it's already summer! Then the rain began to fall. I stood under an overhang and watched as huge, cold, splashing, drops plunged through the warm air. Now it not only felt like summer, it *smelled* like summer.

You have smelled it, too: that sharp, pleasant, *green* scent of rain on dry earth. Those same wonderful odors will even rise from concrete and asphalt. This smell has a fancy name and also a biological explanation. The name is "petrichor," which comes from the Greek words for rock (*petra*) and for the fluid that flows in the veins of the gods in Greek mythology (*ichor*). You are smelling the blood of the gods sprayed up from the rocks. Wiktionary defines it as "the distinctive scent which accompanies the first rain after a long, warm, dry spell."

This wonderful word was coined in 1964 by Isabel Joy Bear and R. G. Thomas, two researchers in Australia who discovered that the scent originates from an oil that plants produce during dry spells to delay seed germination and early plant growth. This may be an adaptation plants use to limit competition during times of low moisture. Rain washes the oil away, stimulating germination and growth. Some biologists suspect that petrichor—washed into streams by rain—signals spawning time for freshwater fish. During dry spells, the oil may also be absorbed by rocks and soils. Falling raindrops liberate the compounds and fling them into the air we breathe.

The rain tapered off, and I walked down the street

on my errands. From the bare soil in expectant flower gardens, another scent rose to meet my nose. This earthy aroma is characteristic of healthy, post-rain soils, and sometimes finds its way into perfumes. The name for this scent, "geosmin," also has a Greek origin (combining the words for earth and smell) and a biological explanation.

Geosmin, an organic compound, is produced by several classes of microbes in the soil, including cyanobacteria (blue-green algae) and actinobacteria (especially *Streptomyces,* which are important to medicine as a source for antibacterial and antifungal agents as well as anticancer drugs). The organisms thrive when the conditions are damp and warm, and create geosmin as a byproduct of living. In an effort to reproduce before they dry out, the bacteria also release geosmin-scented spores. Rain flings these compounds into the air, just as it does with petrichor, and we smell "earth."

Smelling that wonderful earthy aroma is one thing, but tasting it is quite another. Beets, some wines, and bottom-feeding fish like catfish and carp all derive their characteristic earthy flavor from geosmin. Some folks like it and others don't. Even the water we drink can be tainted with the flavor, though it will not hurt you. Human taste buds are very sensitive to geosmin, and the average person can detect it at a concentration of 0.7 parts per billion. The human nose is even more sensitive and can detect geosmin at concentrations as low as five parts per trillion.

In deserts the presence of geosmin usually indicates water. Camels may follow the scent to an oasis and disperse the spores to new places on their travels. Some cacti scent their flowers with geosmin, thereby tricking thirsty insects into serving as pollinators.

In Australia aboriginal people associate petrichor and geosmin with the first life-giving rains of the wet season and with the color green. This smell is so important to them that that they rub geosmin perfume onto their bodies to serve as a symbolic connection between body and landscape. According to research done at the University of Queensland, "The odor is believed to be protective and cleansing, linking present generations to their ancestors."[9]

Without rain, we could not smell petrichor, blood of the gods, and geosmin, the scent of the earth, and have this link to generations past. Without rain, we could not smell summer.

Soon the clouds thinned and dispersed, the pavement dried, and the sun shone. The smell of summer lingered on the breeze, and lilac buds began bursting with green in their effort to catch up.

SUMMER

Tilt and Whirl

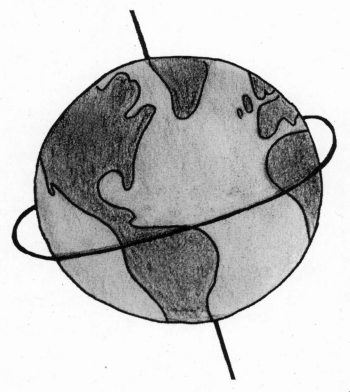

Brooke Sapper, age 16

We are now absorbing more energy from the Sun than we will at any other time of year. Plants sense it, and they grow furiously—photosynthesizing like crazy—before cool weather and lower sun angles return them to winter dormancy. Bees drone lazily in the late afternoon sunshine. A rainbow of flowers blooms along roads, in gardens, and on Hawaiian shirts. Some of the shyer birds have quieted down, while vireos and thrushes still sing their hearts out in their breeding territories. Loons carry fluffy chicks on their checkered backs. Fox kits play and sun themselves outside the den. Mosquitoes buzz in our ears, and shimmering dragonflies come to our rescue.

In this season of growth and vitality, it is easy to forget how stunning fall colors can be or how the forest looked covered in snowdrifts. Every season has its own roses and thorns, and they are all made possible by the tilt of the Earth on its axis.

The Earth's axis is an imaginary line going right through our planet between the north and south poles. The axis tilts 23.5 degrees from the plane of the Earth's orbit around the Sun. For several months of the year, the half of the Earth that angles toward the Sun receives more direct rays and longer hours of sunlight than the other half. Throughout spring our days lengthen minute by minute until we reach the summer solstice. On this day the Sun reaches its northernmost point on our horizon and prepares to journey back south toward winter darkness.

Without the tilt of the Earth's axis, our day length would not change, Alaska would have perpetual twilight, and we would not have the wonderful variety of the four seasons. Instead, two slightly different seasons might emerge based on the distance of the Earth from the Sun. Our elliptical orbit takes us farthest from the Sun (to a point known as the aphelion) around July 3. The perihelion, or the closest point in our orbit, happens around January 4. The difference between the two distances is about 3,000,000 miles, a variation of only about 3 percent. This causes a minor change in the amount of energy from the Sun that reaches Earth, and would not lead to our rainbow of seasons by itself.

While the tilt of the Earth has a big impact on our lives, the tilt itself may have been caused by a large impact. One theory suggests that a huge chunk of space dirt in the early solar system may have slammed into the still-molten Earth—ejecting material that would become the Moon.

Although the word *solstice* derives from a combination of Latin words meaning "sun" + "to stand still," the solstice is not constant over the years. The tilt of the Earth's axis changes by 2.4 degrees (between 22.1 and 24.5 degrees) over 41,000 years. We are comfortably in the middle of that range right now. When the Earth tilts less, the Sun is lower on the horizon in the summer and higher in winter. Summers are cooler and winters are warmer. This changing tilt is one of several large-scale factors influencing the advance and retreat of glaciers over millennia.

Glaciers shaped our landscape and the seasons decorate it. Both owe some thanks to the tilt of the Earth on our axis. Happy solstice!

Little White Flowers

Mike Nechuta

The bright colors of newly opened flowers carpet the road ditches, and this makes riding my bike a little more dangerous. I am chancing skinned elbows and broken bones as I crane my neck to attempt ride-by plant identification or swerve onto the soft shoulder to get a better look. The risk is worth it to greet old friends.

Sometimes in February, when the ski tracks on the Birkie trails are just perfect, I wish it could always be ski season. Then summer arrives in all its glory. In any season I love seeing a delicate dusting of white in the ditches and forests. Of course, right now the white dusting is flower petals instead of snowflakes.

Three species of white flowers stand out in my mind in early summer. Starflower is one. They are aptly named, since their white petals reflect light so brightly that they seem to glow from within and overexpose any photo I take of them. This low plant has a whorl of lanceolate (long, narrow, but wider in the middle) leaves with many delicate veins. Up to three flowers seem to float above the whorl on slender pedicels. What makes this flower truly unusual is the number of petals. Sets of seven are rare in nature.

Often growing nearby in the sun-dappled edges of northern woods are Canada mayflowers, sometimes called false lily of the valley. A shady patch of their small oval leaves may bear no flowers at all. Sometimes just a few plants in a patch will grow a taller stem with two or three leaves and a spike of snowflake-like white flowers. The single leaves may help provide a "chosen plant" with the added energy it needs to bloom and set seed. Since the plants in a patch are clones connected by underground stems, all the little sugar factories can work together. As hardy Northwoods residents know, teamwork is necessary in the face of poor soil and short summers.

The third white flower that caught my eye has a couple

tricks up its leaves or, rather, in the flowers themselves. Bunchberry is the smallest plant in the dogwood family. With radiant white flowers in the summer and brilliant red bunches of berries in the fall, this common plant is always a treat to see. And it harbors more excitement than meets the eye! The four white things masquerading as petals are actually sepals. Sepals are often just small green leaves that cup a flower. While the sepals of bunchberry flowers are unusually showy, the true petals in the center flower cluster are unusually dinky.

Small though they may be, each tiny flower comes equipped with a catapult. When a flower is ready, the lightest touch of a potential pollinator's foot will trigger the petals to burst open in less than a millisecond. This triggers the stamens to release and fling pollen grains with the force of a huge explosive.

According to a study published in the journal *Nature*:

> Bunchberry stamens are designed like miniature medieval trebuchets—specialized catapults that maximize throwing distance by having the payload (pollen in the anther) attached to the throwing arm (filament) by a hinge or flexible strap (thin vascular strand connecting the anther to the filament tip). This floral trebuchet enables stamens to propel pollen upwards faster than would a simple catapult. After the petals open, the bent filaments unfold, releasing elastic energy. The tip of the filament follows an arc, but the rotation of the anther about the filament tip

allows it to accelerate pollen upwards to its maximum
vertical speed, and the pollen is released only as it
starts to accelerate horizontally.[1]

The pollen experiences 800 times the acceleration that
the Space Shuttle does during lift-off and zooms to more
than ten times the height of the flower. From this lofty
height of 2.5 cm, the pollen grains can be caught by the
wind. Or the soaring pollen might smack into a bee and
travel to a different flower that way. Bunchberries cannot
self-pollinate, so this cross-pollination is necessary.

Flowers like these are worth a little swerving as I ride
down the road. Those who are risk averse may choose to
walk instead. In either case, drivers should be alert and
give a wide berth to the many people out enjoying the
wildflower gallery along the roadsides.

A Kid's Eye View

Donna Post

As the six kids gathered at the river landing, I saw looks of shyness, uncertainty, and excitement. The dryland paddling lesson brought looks of concentration and some confusion, and then boredom when they got it. As John Kudlas, a favorite river ecology instructor, taught about water quality, the faces of these mostly sixth and seventh graders showed focused interest. Here in a classroom without walls, I could see them learning.

This was the second annual overnight canoe trip down the Namekagon River for kids ages 12–18. The trip is a partnership between the Cable Natural History Museum, the National Park Service, and Canoes on Wheels. Just as before, we caught macroinvertebrates (the immature stages of insects that spend part of their life in the water before gaining wings and flight), and thankfully, the results still showed that the river is healthy.

As we paddled, I noticed marsh marigolds in bloom, scouring rushes starting to poke up through the water surface, and a couple dragonflies. Birds sang from every bush and tree in a cacophony of joy (and aggression, alarm, and plain chattiness).

I marveled at the bald eagle, sitting calmly in the white pine as we floated underneath. I noticed the power and grace with which the great blue heron rose from its hunting spot. I observed many aquatic plants just barely breaking the river's surface.

But what did the kids see? Sometimes I worry that in this age of television, video games, and the Internet, kids will lose interest in nature and lose the ability to notice things in the unfamiliar complexity of the wild.

So I was excited when, at the campsite on our second morning, the kids each took a small digital camera out of the dry bag and eagerly disappeared into the woods to take photos. Besides giving them an excuse to look closer, compose a frame, and enter the Museum's photo contest, it also gave me a glimpse through their eyes.

What did they notice? The first photos on each memory card showed smiling faces as the kids "labeled" their cameras with a self-portrait. Then came the images of sparkling water and green trees, sunlight glinting off the rapids that the kids were all eager to run, and the river disappearing around a corner into the great unknown.

The photos showed close-ups of bugs—a dragonfly and stonefly that came to visit our picnic table. This was neat because they had found the aquatic nymphs of each insect with John the day before. One photo even showed a backlit oak leaf, its veins and chlorophyll glowing in the morning sun.

The fascinating patterns in a patch of jewelweed leaves must have captured the attention of one boy who used their juicy stems to soothe mosquito bites. His observant eye also caught psychedelic reflections of light and leaves on a pool of water between three rocks.

There was a proud angler, pole and tackle box in hand; also his sister, stretched out on her belly taking photos from an ant's eye view. On her camera, we found a photo of the grass jungle, each delicate seed head silhouetted against the clear, blue sky.

For a different view, several kids looked up into the trees and caught the magnificence of old growth white pines reaching their gnarled branches to the sky. Then they looked down and captured gaywings (small, hot-pink wildflowers) in ethereal morning light and pure-white starflowers against the backdrop of a fallen log.

Some photos were blurry, a few were crooked, and one included the photographer's thumb, but overall, I was thrilled. These kids could still see nature. They will be our next generation of scientists, conservationists, journalists, and engineers. Their ability to see nature will ensure that it is not overlooked.

Magic on the River

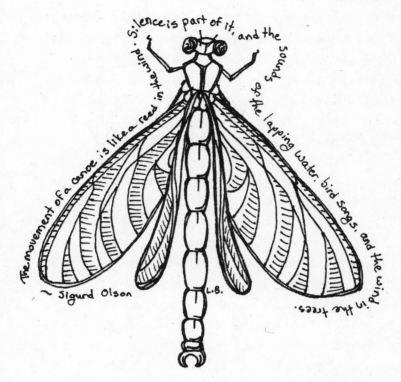

The movement of a canoe is like a reed in the wind. Silence is part of it, and the sounds of the lapping water, bird songs, and the wind in the trees.

~ Sigurd Olson

L.B.

Laura Berlage

"There is magic in the feel of a paddle and the movement of a canoe, a magic compounded of distance, adventure, solitude, and peace."[2] —Sigurd Olson

A few weeks ago, I had the pleasure of seeing six boys come alive on a canoe trip down the river. As we launched from the Cable Wayside Landing, I could sense in them the thrill of adventure. The braided stream channels of the Namekagon River wove their magic around the boys. Every experience, from catching crayfish to casting with fly rods to exploring the campsite, seemed to draw out their spark just as they drew sparks with flint and steel.

This morning at the same landing, I launched those same red canoes with a new group of people. As the sun climbed into a cloudless sky, grandparents, parents, and kids pushed off on a new adventure. Sigurd Olson believed that canoes are "the open door to waterways of ages past,"[3] and Jean Schaeppi, a National Park Service historian with the Saint Croix National Scenic Riverway, prepared us to paddle through that portal.

As Jean spread out the old explorers' and surveyors' maps at the landing, a story unfolded, too. First were the sparse, hand-drawn accounts of early explorers with oddly shaped lakes and enough blank spots to satisfy Aldo Leopold. ("Of what avail are forty freedoms without a blank space on the map?"[4]) Next came the neatly divided surveyors' maps showing a checkerboard of ownership between logging companies and railroads. Finally, there were sketches from old-timers, remembering for posterity the neighbors, farms, and towns of their youth. The final map that Jean handed out was the official National Park Service map of the river, with river mileage, campsites, landings, and roads all accurately marked.

The river has gone through many changes over its lifespan. Nature is reclaiming the last traces of railroad trestles, homesites, and logging dams. Majestic pines, once seedlings in extensive clearcuts, tower along the riverbanks once more. The cultural history of this river continues to evolve and now includes the legacy of visionary politicians who protected it as a National Scenic Riverway. Today the beauty of this place belongs to us all.

With a ten-year-old as my bow paddler and her younger brother as "wildlife spotter" in the middle of the canoe, we enjoyed the freedom of a day spent in nature. Ebony jewelwing damselflies fluttered around the boat and along the shores. The exquisite beauty of their solid-black wings and iridescent green bodies added a spark of wonder to the landscape. Their adult form, twinkling in the bright sunlight, was in stark contrast to their immature nymph stage.

Looking for the whole story, the kids and I picked up rocks in the river's riffles. Clinging to the dark undersides were alien-like creatures with six sprawling legs, two antennae, and three tails. These mossy-brown damselfly nymphs will feed voraciously in the water for several months before climbing a blade of grass, splitting their exoskeletons down the back, and flying away as shimmering adults. The magic of metamorphosis is not rare in nature.

The spin of life cycles, the march of time, and even the flow of a river, all remind us that change is constant. Still, we remain connected to the past. On the Namekagon River, this includes the damselflies as well as early peoples, explorers, loggers, residents, and recreationists, all with their own stories. Sigurd Olson believed that "when a man is part of his canoe, he is part of all that canoes have ever known."[5] That is the magic of the river.

Mosquitoes

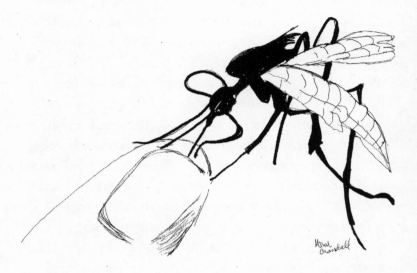

Mimi Crandall

My morning bike commute started out quietly. As the sun rose higher, a few vociferous birds broke the stillness, shouting their exuberant morning songs: "I'm alive! I made it through the night! This is still my territory! I love you, dear! I'm alive!"

Slowly another sound penetrated my pedaling meditation—the squeak of a dry chain. I pulled over onto the grassy shoulder of my rural town road to get out the chain lube. As my tire hit the grass, a cloud of mosquitoes rose with a hum. This sound was far worse than the squeaking of the chain.

A leisurely maintenance break quickly morphed into a NASCAR-style pit stop as I raced against the bugs. Mosquitoes flew behind my sunglasses and landed on every warm surface. Almost more annoying than their bites or their humming was the soft breeze as their wings brushed against my skin. I slapped a few, their bodies crushing easily.

Within a few seconds, I leaped back onto my bike and took off like a shot, as if chased by the devil himself. I sighed in relief as the soundscape returned to morning birdsongs, the stiff breeze in my face, and the hum of my tires on the road.

"Oh the mosquitoes, aren't they just awful this year?" On the street and in the office, mosquitoes are the hot topic. They have almost replaced the weather as our default conversation, except that the weather often determines when the bugs are at their worst, so it cannot be ignored completely. We all have horror stories and love to share.

Inevitably, someone asks, "What good are mosquitoes anyway?"

The negative aspects of mosquitoes are easy to list: they leave itchy welts, create sleep-depriving noise, and are disease vectors for malaria, yellow fever, and dengue fever, to name just a few. In Alaska mosquitoes form swarms thick enough to asphyxiate caribou. But we in the Northwoods are luckier. According to the Wisconsin Department of Health Services, few mosquitoes actually carry West Nile virus, and less than one percent of people infected with the virus become seriously ill.

Of the 3,500 named species of mosquito, only a couple of hundred bite or bother humans. "Mosquitoes have been on Earth for more than 100 million years," says mosquito researcher Jittawadee Murphy, "and they have coevolved with so many species along the way."[6]

Mosquito adults are food for an astounding variety of birds, insects, spiders, salamanders, lizards, and frogs. From northern Canada to Russia, there is a brief annual period in which mosquitoes are extraordinarily abundant. Bruce Harrison, an entomologist at the North Carolina Department of Environment and Natural Resources, estimates that the number of migratory birds that nest in the tundra could drop by more than 50 percent if all mosquitoes miraculously disappeared.[7]

While we don't have quite the mosquito or the bird population that the Arctic does, the warblers, vireos, flycatchers, swallows, and other summer birds that serenaded me to work eat a fair number of the pesky insects.

Dragonflies also do their best to reduce the number of mosquitoes. They are natural enemies of mosquitoes in all their life stages. The aquatic nymphs of dragonflies eat the aquatic larvae of mosquitoes, as do plenty of fish. Dragonfly adults swoop acrobatically, catching mosquitoes in their basket-like legs, and eating their own weight in mosquito burgers every 30 minutes. Mosquito biomass magically becomes a swarm of shimmering dragonflies.

If you have a hard time "becoming one" with the

mosquitoes, there are a few things you can do to make yourself a less-appealing blood meal. Mosquitoes gravitate toward carbon dioxide, heat, lactic acid, smells in your sweat, sweet fruity or floral scents, and dark colors. So you should relax quietly in light-colored clothing, breathe lightly, and use unscented bath products. Unfortunately, our genetics make up about 85 percent of our susceptibility to mosquito bites, so you might just be doomed to itching while your friend is unaffected.

To further deter mosquitos, keep a fan blowing on you (mosquitoes are weak fliers), cover up your scent with a natural bug repellent like citronella or lemon eucalyptus, and avoid their active periods at dawn and dusk. DEET is the longest-lasting effective mosquito repellent, but it is caustic to plastic and other synthetic materials, so use it wisely.

Unsurprisingly, mosquitoes have their own chemical defenses. A female mosquito's saliva (since only they and not males eat blood) contains compounds that deter vascular constriction, blood clotting, and platelet aggregation, and are being researched as treatments for cardiovascular disease. Perhaps that may someday absolve them in our hearts.

If a hungry female mosquito manages to catch up to your frantic pedaling, break through your defenses, and suck some blood, take comfort in knowing that it connects you to the wonderful web of nature.

Wolf Chills

Colleen McCarty

Sometimes, when the temperature rises above 80 degrees, and the humidity hovers around 100 percent, I have to imagine myself in a happier, cooler place. You might be a heat-loving fan of summer, and I am too, sometimes. But when the breeze dies, the bugs flock, and the sweat drips, I find myself dreaming of a snowy wonderland.

On those days I'll flip through old photos to help jog my memories of winter. Here's me on snowshoes with a frozen elk leg strapped to my pack, towering mountains in the background. Here's me, bundled so tightly that barely an inch of skin shows, scarf and hat crusted with driven snow, sitting on the top of a butte near a spotting scope. You can't tell from the photo, but my fingers and toes are numb.

You may think this sounds like pure misery—and I have to admit, there were moments—but it was also one of the most amazing experiences of my life. Those photos are from my month in Yellowstone National Park as a volunteer with the Yellowstone Wolf Project. Every March since the wolves were reintroduced to Yellowstone in 1995, paid and volunteer researchers have collected data on the behavior and biology of the wolves.

On a typical day, my team of three would wake up before the sun and drive our Suburban into the park. An "omni" antenna mounted to the roof of the vehicle received signals from the wolves' radio collars from all directions. If we heard a beep from one of the Oxbow Creek Pack's four collars, we would pull over at the nearest observation point and use the directional or "H" antenna to pinpoint which direction to look. Then we would set up our spotting scopes and scan the rugged landscape for the fifteen members of our pack.

Once we spotted the wolves, our job was to keep them in view for as long as possible and to record every aspect of their behavior by the minute. Talking into little personal recorders, we sounded like this: 7:02 a.m. SLEEP. . . . 7:03 a.m. REST. . . . 7:10 a.m. MILL. . . . 7:11 a.m. RALLY. . . . 7:13 a.m. HOWL. . . . 7:15 a.m. TRAVEL. For 50 percent of the time that we had them in view, our pack was either resting (heads up) or sleeping (heads down).

The excitement came when they rallied and howled. This usually meant that the pack was getting ready to travel and hunt. They loped across the hillsides single file, testing elk among the pine trees. Generally, if an elk stood its ground, the pack would move on. Once I watched as a group of pups surprised a herd of cow elk who panicked and broke into a run. Deep, crusty snow forced the elk to run single file in packed game trails, and the wolves gave chase. Within seconds, the wolves had brought down a cow at the back of the line, and the rest of the herd was out of sight.

After a few days of watching the wolves and then the scavengers turn her body into theirs, we snowshoed in to collect data on the kill. It was soon apparent why she had gone down: one of her legs had broken and healed, and her bone marrow was pink and jellylike, an indication of malnutrition.

It was amazing to watch nature in her finest in the first-ever national park. Bald eagles, golden eagles, magpies, ravens, red foxes, coyotes, and even grizzly bears all feasted on the wolves' scraps. Herds of elk, bighorn sheep, mountain goats, bison, and pronghorns moved through the snowy hills and plains. The sun glowed red on the horizon twice a day, unless it was blotted out by swirling snow.

One of the most thrilling events took place near our observation point above Geode Marsh. I was hiking along a side hill in the swirling snow, when over the whoosh of the wind I heard a mournful cry. It was soon joined by a chorus of rising howls that made the very air around me shiver.

Much nicer than 85 degrees with 95 percent humidity!

Loon Language

Reese Leann Gbur, age 10

The mournful wail of a common loon echoes across the glassy water. From a nearby lake, another loon replies with the same smooth cry. The loons are keeping track of one another, maybe as neighbors, maybe as mates, maybe as rivals.

Sometimes the still night air is pierced by the maniacal, laughing yodels of two male loons. This signifies a territorial battle. Home territory means a lot to loons. The longer a male resides in the same territory, the greater his chance of raising chicks to adulthood. The resident male will fight to the death if necessary to defend his island, lake, or bay. Females are just as tied to territory. Even if the invading male wins, the resident female will stay on the territory with the new male.

An invading loon, looking for his own place to raise a family, will fly over an occupied territory and first give the wavering tremolo flight call. If the resident male is willing to fight for the prime real estate, he will reply with a yodel. The invading loon can tell approximately how big the defender is by the lowest note in the yodel and use this information to decide whether a fight is in his favor or not. If he chooses to fight, the invader replies with his own unique yodel. Loons can tell each other apart by their calls, and even third graders can tell loons apart by looking at sonograms of their yodels!

Once a territory and mate are secured, the male loon chooses a nest site hidden in tall vegetation near the water. The female builds the nest by pulling plants around her body to form a low bowl. After that, they share parenting duties fifty-fifty. Alternating incubating and eating, they wait for 26–31 days until the two eggs hatch a day apart.

The parents communicate with the chicks using a soft, short "hoot." If eagles are present, the parents may give a special version of a wail. Bald eagles are a known predator of loons, and the alarm call tells the chicks to "DIVE NOW!"

Eagles are not the only danger for loon chicks. Gulls are also nest raiders. In the Boundary Waters Canoe Area Wilderness, fish guts left by anglers allowed the population of gulls to increase. More gulls meant fewer loons. In recent years officials have been encouraging anglers to dispose of fish remains in the woods, away from aerial scavengers.

Many anglers enjoy watching loons on their favorite lakes, while others see the loons as competition. Loons mostly eat smaller fish like yellow perch and do not have a significant impact on most game fish. Humans can negatively affect loons in several ways, though. Excessive wakes near nesting sites can knock eggs into the water. Snagged fishhooks and line can entangle many kinds of wildlife. Lead sinkers are also a major issue.

Loons do not have teeth, and neither do they have a mechanism like owls to cough up pellets of undigested hard parts. The scales and bones of fish have to go all the way through their digestive system. To achieve that, loons have muscular gizzards, and they ingest small, round rocks to help pulverize their food. Unfortunately, lead sinkers look like perfect gizzard stones. Many loons and other wildlife die a prolonged and painful death by lead poisoning every year.

Lead is not the only toxin we introduce into lakes. Every year around the Fourth of July, and sometimes throughout the summer, we sprinkle a wide assortment of toxic elements into the lakes. We are so awed by the spectacle of beautiful fireworks reflecting on the water that we do not think about the morning after. The noise of the explosions can frighten loons off their nests—leaving the eggs open to predators. Plastic casings from fireworks can sneak into the food chain, causing malnutrition. Plus, those interesting, but sometimes carcinogenic elements in the fireworks—the ones that make cool colors when they burn—can end up in the lake.

In July we can see days-old chicks so fluffy they pop up like corks and awkward teenage chicks just learning to dive. Some loons are still incubating eggs—trying to nest for a second or third time after their first attempts were foiled by thunderstorms, raccoon raids, or other bad luck. Please try not to make their tough parenting job any harder!

Loons are icons of our beloved Northwoods. Their sight and songs bring joy to many residents and visitors of the area. As you enjoy their home, please consider how your behavior can affect them.

Kale: Servant or Master?

Mimi Crandall

Hot sun beat down on my neck as I crouched in the dirt, pulling thin blades of quack grass from out between my kale plants. Weed by weed, I slowly reached the end of the row, stood up, and stretched my back. A quick survey showed that my work was not even close to being done. My plot at the brand-new Cable Community Farm had only recently been sheep pasture, and even after three rounds of tillage, quack grass roots still run deep.

The kale looked relaxed and happy, though, in its spacious row. For a moment, I felt a twinge of resentment. Why does kale get to just sit there and grow, doing the only thing it really wants to do, while I have to toil away, tilling the soil, planting the seeds, watering the garden, and weeding away any competitors? By offering up its tasty, nutritious leaves, the kale has seduced me into catering to its every whim.

"The garden suddenly appeared before me in a whole new light, the manifold delights it offered to the eye and nose and tongue no longer quite so innocent or passive. All these plants, which I'd always regarded as the objects of my desire, were also, I realized, subjects, acting on me, getting me to do things for them they couldn't do for themselves,"[8] Michael Pollan writes in his excellent book, *The Botany of Desire*.

When I first found Pollan's book on a friend's coffee table and read the introduction, it completely changed the way I think about domesticated plants. Although I love to eat kale and almost every other fruit and vegetable, I have always had more respect, more reverence, for native plants. If you think about it, though, everything in our gardens started in the wild somewhere, once upon a time.

Michael Pollan flips our perception of plants upside down and asks us to think about domestication "as something plants have done to us—a clever strategy for advancing their own interests."[9] Their own interest, as with every living thing, is to make more copies of themselves, to reproduce.

Just as plants use nectar to trick bees into transporting their pollen, plants bribe us with sweet fruits, crunchy leaves, nutritious seeds, and beautiful flowers. In return, we choose the seeds of their genetic kin to be collected, sold, and replanted year after year. We bring them to a good habitat, protect them from pests, reduce their competition with other plants, and make sure that their every need is met.

The tastiest, most prolific varieties (think Brandywine tomatoes, Provider bush beans, or my Winterbor kale . . . what's your favorite?) are first developed through selective breeding and then replanted over and over again. In the meantime, the quack grass and other weeds are tilled under, pulled out, and repeatedly beaten back. Pollan says, "Our desires are simply more grist for evolution's mills, no different from a change in the weather: a peril for some species, and opportunity for others."[10]

When I write about nature, I usually choose to write about wild things out in the woods. But, as Pollan observes, "Nature is not only to be found 'out there'; it is also 'in here,' in the apple and the potato, in the garden and the kitchen . . ." My relationship with nature does not stop at the garden gate. In fact, by planting, nurturing, and eating these other living beings, I develop an even more intimate connection with nature, and weave myself more fully into the "reciprocal web of life that is Earth."[11]

Yes, kale and other vegetables have persuaded me to pamper them, but I do receive gifts in return, just like the bee on the rose bush. Instead of a hive full of honey, I will survive winter with a freezer full of kale.

Web of Intrigue

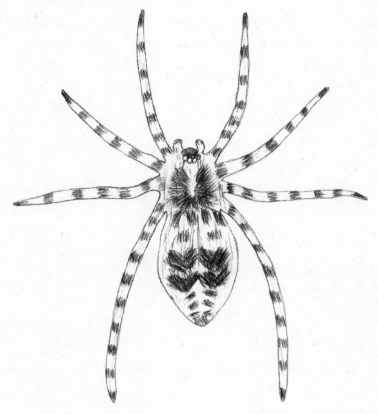

Kellie Solberg

Fog hung thick over the lake, and early morning light filtered through the trees. I bent low in front of my favorite lakeside window, touching my toes and enjoying the stretch. As I rose up and extended my arms overhead, a dark shape in the corner of the window caught my eye.

On the outside of the screen was an enormous spider. Including legs, it had to be at least two inches across.

Spiders are amazing creatures, but I can't escape a tiny bit of innate fear triggered by the largest ones. Still, in the spirit of my yoga practice, I silently appreciated this spider for eating some of the bugs trying to sneak into the house to eat *me*! Then, I glanced at the adjacent window and saw the silhouette of a spider twice the size of the first one.

Female dark fishing spiders are the largest spiders regularly found in the Northwoods. This particular female was about as big as they come, with a leg span of almost four inches. The first, smaller spider must have been a male, since they are about half the size of females. As their name implies, most fishing spiders live near water. Dark fishing spiders stray farther from water than other species of fishing spiders and are often found near docks, in wet woods, and in basements.

With dark and light chevron patterns on their large, oval abdomens, and dark and light stripes encircling their legs, these spiders are quite striking. My roommates had assumed these were wolf spiders, but wolf spiders don't get as large overall, and they have much bigger eyes. The difference in the eye size of the two families is indiciatve of their hunting techniques.

Wolf spiders are visual hunters who pounce on prey by day and night. Fishing spiders use a range of vibration-detecting organs, including very sensitive hairs on their legs and feet to sense prey. I think that my spiders were sensing vibrations on the window screen. Other species of these hairy hunters sense their prey's movement through vibrations on the water's surface. Their eyes are only secondary, and they do not spin webs.

Dark fishing spiders do, however, spin a web of intrigue with their odd mating habits. The reproductive techniques of all spiders seem a little strange from a human perspective. Male spiders produce semen in testes on their abdomen, then spin a sperm web, fill it with sperm, and suck the sperm up into their pedipalps, which are antenna-like sensory organs near the spider's face. The sperm inflates the pedipalps.

The male does the appropriate love dance, climbs up on the female, inserts one of his pedipalps into her genital opening, and deposits the sperm.

Here is where the dark fishing spider gets peculiar. A recent study revealed that for the male, mating is like committing suicide. "The act of sperm transfer is triggering this cascade of death," says Steven Schwartz, a behavioral ecologist at the University of Nebraska. "Once that button is pushed, it's lights out."[12] The male dark fishing spider's legs curl up, and he becomes immobile.

If the male dark fishing spider is lucky, the female will eat him, become satiated, and not mate with other males. This benefits the deceased male by ensuring that he will be the father of her spider babies. If he isn't lucky, he dies within a couple of hours and the female goes on her merry way.

As the rising sun illuminates my window, I see the

spiders on my windows in a new light. I respect the complexity of a relationship I can't fully understand.

"Have compassion for all beings, rich and poor alike; each has their suffering." —Buddha

Partnerships in Light and Dark

Donna Post

Breaking out of the dense canopy onto a rocky cliff, I glanced first at the stunning view of Lake Superior, then to the shrubs around my feet. The color of the day was deep blue. This section of the Superior Hiking Trail is known as "Blueberry Ridge," and not without cause. Blueberries can survive in this hot sun and poor soil where many plants cannot, and in fact, this is where blueberries thrive. I noticed blueberry plants in the deeply shaded forest— but not a single berry. Now with the morning sun in my eyes, I picked steadily from clusters of wild candy.

Blueberry plants are sugar factories. They capture the plentiful sunlight energy and use it to manufacture fructose from water and carbon dioxide. But neither a plant nor a berry-picking naturalist can live on sugar alone. In this thin, rocky soil, getting the right suite of nutrients and water for growth can be tough. Blueberry plants have helpers, though, just like many other plants in their heath family.

If a blueberry root is stained with dye and viewed through a microscope, thin strands of fungal hyphae coiled within the root cells and extending as thin threads outside the root become visible. The hyphae act like root extensions, drawing in nutrients and water from beyond the typical reach of the blueberry. The fungus—a decomposer—can break down soil components to access nutrients that are otherwise locked away. The blueberry pays for this service by giving the fungus little sugar snacks.

The blueberry's mycorrhizal (fungus-root) relationship is wholesome compared to some of its close kin. Those shady cousins have a more deceitful way to make a living.

Back in the forest, layer upon layer of leaves filter out most of the noontime sun before it reaches the forest floor. Red-capped *Russula* mushrooms with white stalks brighten up the brown leaf litter. The few understory plants that can survive here must have low energy needs and an ability to capture even fleeting glimmers of sun. Or they might be thieves.

While a stereotypical burglar dresses in all black, one bandit shines with the translucent white glow of innocence. Sometimes called Indian pipe, ghost plant, or corpse plant, the cluster of eight-inch-tall flower stalks is a cousin of blueberries and cranberries who takes mycorrhizal relationships to the extreme. Indian pipe has no chlorophyll to make it green, and it cannot photosynthesize. It does not need to make food, because this myco-parasitic plant is getting ALL of its food from a fungus.

Some of Indian pipe's most common fungal providers are *Russulas*, those pretty red mushrooms that are popping up everywhere in summer. These fungi are engaged in their own mycorrhizal relationship with the trees, and are currently exchanging micro-nutrients and water for the sweet products of photosynthesis. Indian pipe fools the fungus into thinking they are forming a mycorrhizal relationship. Then it steals the sugars, giving nothing in return. Scientists have traced this one-way flow of sugars by introducing radioactive carbon into tree leaves, then watching it flow down through the *Russula* and out into the Indian pipe, where it stays.

In both sunlight and shadow, the intricate relationships of nature fill our lives with sweetness and beauty.

Have You Ever Smelled a Garter Snake?

Ayla Baussan, age 6

Have you ever smelled a garter snake? A foul, sweetish odor permeated the screen porch and clung to my hands as we passed the small snake around. The scent is a defense mechanism that makes garter snakes less appetizing to potential predators.

The twelve middle school kids on the field trip were not deterred, and the snake calmed down as we examined it.

One student in particular was reluctant to pass the snake on and watched, mesmerized, as the yellow and black creature twined around his hands and even slithered up his sleeve.

My first clear memory of a garter snake is from fourth grade, when Clayton County Iowa naturalist Karen Newbern gave a program in the school library. There, on the pea-green, low-pile carpet, the snake pooped. It reminded me of a cheeseburger.

Snake feces is a lot like other animal waste. It smells, it is often brown, and it happens as often as the animal eats. Because snakes only have a single utilitarian opening called a cloaca, their poop combines with urea from their kidneys. It is the same with bird poop, where you see the purple berry seeds mixed with white urea. That particular snake had yellow urea that looked just like melted cheese to my young imagination, along with a brown, chunky center.

Today, as we examined the garter snake, retired zoologist and Museum volunteer Ed Moll reminded the kids to hold the snake carefully with two hands. Garter snakes are not constrictors, so they don't cling to you like bull snakes or fox snakes.

Constrictors have strong muscles they use to squeeze their prey to death and then eat it, but garter snakes simply seize prey in their mouth and work it down. This is where their poop starts—as a rodent, frog, slug, earthworm, leech, lizard, amphibian, ant, cricket, frog egg, or toad. Garter snakes are generalist carnivores. They will eat almost anything they can overpower.

While their stinky musk protects garter snakes from being prey, three features of their mouths make it easier for them to be the predator. First, garter snakes have an extra bone between their skull and lower jaw. That bone allows their mouth to open 180 degrees. Second, the two halves of their lower jaw are not fused and can move independently. Finally, their teeth point down their throat.

Garter snakes can open up wide enough to let a toad in and then walk the critter down their throat by using one side of their jaw at a time. Next their ribs flare, and their skin stretches to accommodate the breakfast bulge.

If attempting this with a live and wiggling prey sounds daunting, you may be interested to know that garter snakes, although often thought of as nonvenomous, have a little venom to assist with the process. The venom is in their saliva and seems to flow only after a bit of chewing. The mild toxin helps to stun their prey and is not usually dangerous to humans, unless you are bitten repeatedly and develop an allergy.

After the prey makes it to their belly, snakes will go into a dormant mode and expend as little energy as possible on things other than digestion. Optimal digestion occurs at 86 degrees, as stomach enzymes break down all but the bones, teeth, and feathers of their prey. These hard parts will be excreted as waste . . . and sometimes look like a cheeseburger.

Despite the musky smell on Ed's screen porch, the students sat mesmerized by the snake and its amazing adaptations. Until, that is, one parent chaperone called it a *garden* snake. "There is no such thing!" exclaimed Ed, breaking their trance with a good-natured shout. Hopefully that lesson will linger even longer than the *garter* snake's smell.

The Kingdom of Fungi

Rachel Bunyard, age 15

We explored a magical kingdom yesterday—a kingdom filled with mystery, danger, humor, healing, and beauty— the kingdom of fungi.

Our guide for the mushroom foray was Britt A. Bunyard, PhD, publisher, and editor in chief of *FUNGI* magazine. He gave some quick hints for collecting mushrooms: never use plastic bags, use a knife to dig up the base of the mushroom, and learn your trees. Plastic bags will make the mushrooms sweat and spoil your dinner, the mushroom's base may hold the key to its identification, and certain species of fungi prefer certain species of trees.

The woods at the Forest Lodge Nature Trail, ten miles east of Cable, Wisconsin, are mixed with such a hodgepodge of trees that we simply spread out to scour the whole area. The roots of a pine might be sprouting mushrooms near the base of a maple, while the intervening dead wood and moss hold a variety of mycelia with the potential to grow many species.

Soon the contents of everyone's baskets and bags came together in a rainbow of fungi on a picnic table at the trailhead. Instead of starting with the brilliant orange and yellow specimens, where all of our eyes focused, Britt held up a large, drab chunk of oak bark. Mysterious black shoestrings clung to the furrows on the brown slab. "These are the rhizomorphs of the honey mushroom," he said.

The honey mushroom uses rhizomorphs to spread and infect live trees, live and dead roots, and stumps. The stringy, black, root-like rhizomorphs can grow at a rate of one yard per year. They transport a fungus that can girdle a tree and kill it. The mycelia (the vegetative part of a fungus, consisting of a mass of branching, thread-like hyphae) can lie hidden for years before bursting forth a cluster of choice edible mushrooms.

Just don't mistake the white-spored honey mushroom for the dark-spored, aptly named, deadly galerina.

Death from mushroom poisonings is less common than shark attacks, but Gary Lincoff, author of the *National Audubon Society's Field Guide to North American Mushrooms*, cautions that "any mushroom is edible once." The danger of eating wild mushrooms is sometimes played down by experts. True, only a couple species will actually kill you, but I think the professionals love the feeling of defying death through their own wit and expertise.

To caution us further, Britt pulled another chunk of bark out of his basket, this time with a group of small, globular, light brown fungi attached. "Who recognizes these?" he challenged. "Puffballs!" several of us exclaimed, excited to see an edible we could identify. While somewhat bland, many folks love them fried in butter and garlic.

"No!" interjected Britt, "and this one could kill you." Deaths from the common earth-ball, *Scleroderma citrinum*, are rare, but it does cause severe gastric upset. The tough, scaly skin on these small, rounded, stemless mushrooms makes them look a little like old potatoes. Descriptively, it is sometimes called the pigskin poison puffball. Britt whipped out his European-made mushrooming knife and sliced the earth-ball in half. A thick rind of a slightly different shade of white surrounded creamy flesh, but in the center was a hard, inky purple stain.

If you've eaten the true puffballs, you know that the center must be pure white and undifferentiated. If not, you risk eating a disgusting puffball past its prime or a poisonous look-alike. True puffballs, like the one we thought Britt was showing us, release their spores through a single opening in a cloud of greenish-gray dust. Perhaps this is where they earned their scientific name *Lycoperdon pyriforme*. In Greek *lyco* means wolf, *perdon* means fart, and *pyriforme* means pear-shaped. It is a pear-shaped wolf's fart puffball. Who said mycologists don't have a sense of humor?

While laughter may be the best medicine, some mushrooms are miracle cures in themselves. The chaga, a pathogenic mass of fungal tissue and wood from its birch tree host, is purported to have compounds that can be used to treat cancer, HIV, and diabetes.

The ugly, black and rust-brown mass of the chaga contrasts with the delicate, earth-toned rainbows of turkey tail fungus. We found a log filled with remains of last year's dried and crumpled crop. With fall rains, this common polypore bracket fungus, found throughout the world, will sprout anew. This little wonder has been shown in clinical studies to improve cancer patients' immune systems after chemotherapy.

Some mushrooms heal us just with their unexpected beauty. Shining like jewels, brilliant orange waxy caps poke their tiny heads out of soft moss. Nearby, the scarlet caps of *Russulas* sit atop pure white stems. Under the bark of a tree, a green elfcup fungus imparts its turquoise stain on the wood.

Many gifts await those who explore the magical kingdom of fungi.

Blackberry Receptacles

Donna Post

Reaching through the thorny bramble, my fingers closed on the biggest, juiciest, blackberry I had ever seen. My pail was more than half full, but this berry did not join the crowd. Instead I popped it straight into my mouth, and sweet juice burst into every corner. I love berry season!

Berry season is a time for red fingers and purple tongues. Not just blackberries, but raspberries, serviceberries, and blueberries all contain the pigment anthocyanin, which can be red, purple, or blue depending on the acidity of the fruit. In nature pigments do not just provide color; they also perform important functions. Anthocyanin is useful to plants as a sunscreen and to humans as an antioxidant.

In fact, blackberries' antioxidant capacity ranks near the top of 1,000 antioxidant foods consumed in the United States. They are also notable for their high nutritional contents of dietary fiber, vitamin C, vitamin K, folic acid (a B vitamin), and the essential mineral manganese. Blackberries even retain most of these health benefits through the process of making them into jam and storing them over the winter.

As my pail filled with blackberries (the goal of the day), my mouth often filled with red raspberries, too. These close cousins share the genus *Rubus* in the rose family. Have you ever noticed that when you pluck a raspberry off the plant, there is a little white dome left behind? The matching recess in the berry itself is the perfect size for capping fingertips or hiding sneaky bugs. Blackberries don't share that shape. Their base is flat, and they pluck cleanly off the stem. There is a botanical reason for this.

Raspberries and blackberries begin with very similar flowers. They both have five, white petals that surround an outer ring of many stamens (the pollen-producing organs) and an inner cluster of pistils (the female organs). All these parts are joined at their bases in a structure that botanists call the hypanthium. The hypanthium, in turn, is attached to a flower stalk called the receptacle.

When a pollen grain lands on one of the many stigmas (the tip of the pistil), it travels down a pollen tube to fertilize the ovule (egg) in the ovary. The fertilized ovule becomes the seed, and the ovary develops into a juicy fruit. On raspberries, the tops of the pistils remain as tiny hairs bristling out of each bump on the fruit.

I sometimes marvel at how hard blackberry seeds are when they get stuck between my teeth. Each tiny seed is enclosed in a lignified (woody) case—just like the pit of a peach. The term for this type of fruit with a soft, outer flesh and an hard-shelled seed is a drupe. Cherries are another example of drupes.

When the many pistils in raspberry or blackberry flowers receive pollen, each ovary develops into a mini drupe. The drupelets then fuse together into the many-dimpled fruits we know and love. Thus blackberries and raspberries are not berries at all, but aggregates of drupelets. True berries are simple (not aggregate) fruits that develop from a single ovary. Some examples of true berries include avocados, bananas, blueberries, grapes, tomatoes, watermelons, and pumpkins.

The main difference between the two delicacies I encountered in the thorny bramble is that in addition to fusing all the little drupes together, blackberries incorporate the receptacle (the base of the flower) into the fruit, while raspberries leave their little white cone of a receptacle still attached to the plant.

Botany is fascinating, but at the end of the day, the only receptacles that truly matter are the full pail and my happy belly!

In a Field of Goldenrod: Part I

Lois Nestel

Kids and naturalists wielding bug nets ventured into
the tangle of plants. Sweeping the nets from side to
side among the grasses and flowers, these budding
entomologists soon discovered the diversity of life hiding
in an overgrown field.

Plumes of yellow goldenrod flowers danced in the
breeze next to succulent stalks of common milkweed, and
insects buzzed in the warm sunshine. While goldenrod

flowers get a bad reputation for being the cause of summer allergies, their heavy pollen grains don't actually drift through the air and into our nostrils. Their brilliant yellow flower heads and leafy, green stalks do provide food and shelter for a myriad of insects, and insects were what we hoped to find.

My first catch, since I was one of the participating kids on this bug-collecting expedition, was a beautiful grasshopper with red hind legs. Appropriately named the red-legged grasshopper, *Melanoplus femurrubrum* (from femur = thigh, rubrum = red), it is one of the most common grasshoppers in North America, with the center of its population directly over the Midwest.

Red-legged grasshoppers have good nutrition down pat, eating a variety of plant species in a single meal. Those who feed on just one type of plant, even seemingly nutritious alfalfa, develop health issues and produce fewer eggs. The way they chew is interesting, too. I learned from Mary Oliver's poem "The Summer Day" that grasshoppers move their jaws back and forth to chew!

The chewing action of the goldenrod gall fly, *Eurosta solidaginis*, does more than just facilitate eating. After a female gall fly deposits an egg into the stem of a goldenrod plant, the egg hatches in about ten days, and the larva immediately starts eating the stem from the inside out. The chewing action and the larva's saliva, which is thought to mimic plant hormones, cause the goldenrod's stem to thicken into a dense, round gall. Several of these bright green globes were visible in the field.

Now sliding my bug net over the top of a goldenrod flower (nodding above a swollen gall), I caught a beautiful, tricolored bumblebee, *Bombus ternarius.* I was glad to have a closer look, because I'd seen several on prairie blazing star flowers at the Forest Lodge Nature Trail recently and wondered who they were. These smaller bees tend to forage at the tips of the goldenrod flower clusters, while letting bigger bees occupy the cluster's center.

Looking closely at the center of a goldenrod flower cluster, I noticed a deviation in the pattern of blossoms. Peering closer, the smooth, round body and eight legs of a goldenrod crab spider came into focus. This tiny spider has a short, broad abdomen, and legs that are held outstretched to the side that enable it to move sideways, forward, and back just like a crab.

Goldenrod flowers are a perfect spot for this spider to wait in ambush for bees, wasps, butterflies, moths, and other nectar-seeking insects. To camouflage itself from the eyes of both predators and prey, crab spiders can change from the yellow to white, depending on the color of the flower where they live.

Some consider goldenrod a weed, while others plant it in their gardens. After an hour spent sorting and identifying the diversity of insects trapped by our nets, it is evident that no matter what we think of it, many insects like goldenrod just fine.

And just for the record, it is ragweed—not goldenrod—that makes you sneeze.

In a Field of Goldenrod: Part II

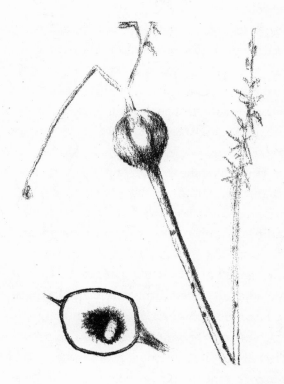

Vivianne Hanke

"Imagine yourself living in a globelike room with greenish walls bulging outward and upward and then arching in to meet above your head," naturalist Edwin Way Teale writes. "Imagine such a room constructed of succulent, edible material, forming a house that at once provides food and shelter, plenty and protection. That is what you would find if you traded places with one of those gall insects that now live in the globular swellings on the stem of my hillside goldenrods."[13]

Those galls began their story last spring. After a female goldenrod gall fly, *Eurosta solidaginis,* deposited an egg on the stem of a growing goldenrod plant, the egg hatched in about 10 days. The larva immediately bore down into the stem. The chewing action and the larva's saliva, which is thought to mimic plant hormones, caused the goldenrod's stem to thicken.

Soon runaway cell division triggered by the larva formed a dense, round growth on the stem called a gall. This provided both food and shelter as the larva grew up. After going through three stages, called instars, the larva is ready for winter.

The larva will not leave the gall yet. Instead, it will excavate an exit tunnel in the gall to use in the spring, leaving just the outermost layer as a door. The larva must chew the corridor now because once it pupates into an adult, it will not have chewing mouthparts. The larva will then retreat to the center of the gall and fill its cells with glycerol, a cryoprotectant that protects cells from damage due to freezing.

I often stop to examine dried, brown galls as I ski or snowshoe through snowy fields. If you open a gall in the middle of winter, you may find the larva, surrounded by the debris excavated from the exit tunnel. They make good fish bait and are protein-rich snacks for downy woodpeckers and chickadees.

Downy woodpeckers have a thin, sharp beak that neatly excavates the tough, dry material. Chickadees have blunter beaks and make large messy craters. The size and neatness of the hole indicate which bird attacked the gall. In contrast, the larva's own exit hole (if it makes it through the winter) is tiny and perfectly round, with no rough edges and no concave excavation pit.

Predators help determine the size of the galls. Downy woodpeckers select larger galls to attack, probably hoping for a more substantial grub. In areas where downies are common, flies with smaller galls survive better, and smaller galls are more common.

Birds are not the only creatures who exploit gallfly larvae, though. A parasitic wasp, *Eurytoma gigantea*, uses its long ovipositor to penetrate the gall wall and lay an egg inside. The newborn wasp larva first eats the fly larva and then continues to feed on the gall tissue until it pupates. The length of the wasp's ovipositor restricts her to laying eggs in smaller galls. Therefore, in areas where the wasps are common, galls tend to be larger. Where both downy woodpeckers and wasps are common, middle ground is found.

(To see why goldenrod gall fly larvae appeal to so many predators, I recommend that you taste one for yourself. The concentration of glycerol makes them slightly sweet. I've taught many students who were willing to accept that challenge!)

After two weeks as a pupa in the spring, the new adult gall fly will emerge. Seeking a mate, it will climb up a nearby goldenrod shoot. After mating, the female fly will leave in search of a new goldenrod stem in which to deposit her eggs.

Female gall flies are quite picky about which type of goldenrod to lay their eggs on. Distinct fly "races" prefer certain species of goldenrod. The females can tell goldenrod species apart by tasting the plants with chemical sensors on their feet, antennae, and even in their ovipositors. When a female finds the right plant, she lays an egg or two, and the story beings again.

Once predators, parasites, or metamorphosis empties the galls, they become habitat for a variety of insects. Springtails, wasps, solitary bees, beetles, and ant colonies have been discovered using the galls. Next time when you go for a walk or a ski in a field of goldenrod, take a moment to imagine yourself spending the winter in the globelike room of a goldenrod gall.

Late Summer Song

Carol Werner

The half-mile bike ride to my garden is a pleasure in both the early morning and the early evening. Soft light illuminates fluffy clouds, fresh breezes bring relief from the heat of the day, and the ethereal song of the hermit thrush drifts through the quiet forest. Most birds are done singing for the year. Their chicks are fledged, and males no longer need to defend a territory or attract a mate. The cacophony of early summer is replaced by a few vocal marathoners.

Hermit thrushes are one of the earliest birds to return to the Northwoods in spring, and their beautiful song is a welcome contrast to the gray days of late March. With almost equal vigor, they continue to sing throughout the summer. Their song begins with a thin whistle, followed with a fluty jumble of notes. The fluty quality, and often the impression of a duet as well, comes from the thrush's elaborate sound system.

Amphibians, reptiles, and mammals (including humans) sing using a larynx. Humans generate sound by forcing air through the trachea, causing thin membranes to vibrate. The human larynx only uses about 2 percent of the air that a person exhales. Birds, in contrast, have a syrinx. This set of membranes restricts airflow through the trachea, right where it splits into the two bronchial tubes.

The syrinx is much more efficient than a larynx and can turn almost all of the passing air into sound. This ability is why tiny birds can make gigantic sounds. With the syrinx straddling two separate tubes, each with separate sound-producing membranes, control muscles, and neural connections, thrushes and other birds can produce two sounds at once. Songbirds (including thrushes) can even do their own version of circular breathing by singing out of one side of the syrinx while inhaling quick breaths through the other side.

Not all birds have the same sound system. Both the structure of the syrinx and the training to use it can differ. Thrushes and some other oscine (from the Latin word "to sing") songbirds need to learn their songs. In the suboscine group that includes flycatchers and eastern phoebes, songs are innate. Other birds, like vultures, can hardly make sounds at all.

Many herons only make harsh squawks, but the American bittern makes a loud, guttural, booming, "oog-ka-chuk." Males fill their gullets with air and then release it through a specialized esophagus. The bittern's unique call has led to some entertaining common names, including water-belcher, mire drum, and thunder pumper.

Low sounds, like that of a bittern, travel well in the evening air of wetlands and can be heard at a distance of several miles. This enables scientists to count several types of marsh birds using song surveys.

That's handy because visual surveys of the bittern would be difficult. Long, brown and white vertical stripes on their bellies provide them with excellent camouflage in tall marsh grasses, and they even sway with the wind to make their disguise complete.

Unlike thrushes, bitterns only sing during mating season in the spring. The silence of summer adds to birds' camouflage as they raise their fledglings and molt feathers. The birds that do keep singing, like the hermit thrush, may be conducting singing lessons with their young.

Both hermit thrushes and American bitterns will soon be preparing for migration, and the woods will be even quieter. I may have already heard the last thrush concert for this year. Luckily, there are several hardy birds that stay throughout the year, and the cheerful calls of chickadees will keep both me and the garden company through the winter.

The Woods Are Not Silent

Josie Trossen, 7th grade

All but a few birds have ceased singing even their late summer songs. While we no longer hear the lilting phrases of love and territorial defense jumbled in a cacophonic morning chorus, the woods are not silent.

Daydreaming on a walk the other day, I gradually became aware of darting movements and soft chip notes in the low, leafy trees. A little flock of foraging warblers engaged in a constant conversation of "companion calls." These chips and chirps in a regular back-and-forth rhythm indicate that everything is okay. In late summer different species of warblers flock together, to make use of extra eyes and safety in numbers. Migrants often join with chickadees who serve as local guides to the best restaurants and away from the most dangerous neighborhoods. As they forage for tasty insects and juicy caterpillars, the small birds cannot keep in constant visual contact with each other through the leaves. Companion calls help keep track of every bird in the flock.

Finding food is essential for these little engines who weigh only as much as seven cents. They are on an epic journey. The black-and-white warbler, whom I recognized from its striking stripes and nuthatch-like behavior, is heading for somewhere on its extensive winter range—anywhere from Florida to Venezuela and Colombia. Today must be a stopover day, a time to refuel for the journey ahead.

The other visitors in the flock were drab olive green, the standard color of young warblers and adults in nonbreeding plumage. Birders know them as "confusing fall warblers." I could not identify them to species, but it is a safe bet that they also are heading to somewhere in Central or South America for the winter. The secrets of how birds find their way on this incredible journey remain mostly hidden. They appear to navigate using a variety of cues that include the stars, the Earth's magnetic field, and even smell.

The many-mile migration of these tiny birds is triggered by a combination of factors, including a change in day length, lower temperatures, dwindling food supplies, and genetic predisposition. Since presence or absence of food is not the only or the most important trigger, putting out food for the birds through autumn and winter (even hummingbirds!) will not interrupt their migration.

Warblers come here in the spring to find a space of their own where they can take advantage of long days and feed ravenous youngsters on our plentiful crop of insects. Their songs are the soundtrack of summer. They leave in the fall when the shorter days and freezing temperatures make those same insects much harder to find. Yet the woods are not silent.

As amazing as it is that these tiny creatures can travel 2,000 miles or more twice a year, I also have a deep respect for the year-round residents who make do and even thrive in the bitter (and beautiful) Northern winters. Chickadees, nuthatches, and downy woodpeckers find enough food to fuel their internal fires and seem almost cheerful throughout the wintry months. Thanks to the wonderful diversity of lifestyles in nature, the woods are never silent.

Curiosity

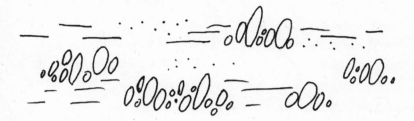

Martin Bevis

Bright summer sunlight trickled through the thick canopy of trees and danced across the shallow stream. Two dozen little feet clad in their oldest shoes tramped through the water, too, somewhat less gracefully than the sun flecks. This was crick stomping at its best: a hot day, cool shade, refreshing water, and a sense of adventure.

I felt like a mother hen at the center of the flock as we moved our way upstream. Instead of pecking at grain, the chicks' hands darted out to pick up this rock or that one. I was always glad when my Girl Scout campers got as excited about rocks as I did. The shallow, flashy nature of the camp's creek meant that on most days several small channels braided themselves through wide gravel bars of interesting rocks. After big thunderstorms, I loved to watch as a torrent of brown water churned and frothed down the creek, revealing an alien landscape to explore as the floodwater receded.

On this particular crick stomp, we brought along an honored guest. A NASA scientist named Owl (a camp name chosen because she liked the nighttime) was in the creek with us. She was part of a NASA outreach program involving girls and science. She led us in activities like creating creatures that could survive in each planet's unique habitat, dissecting candy bars as if they were types of bedrock, and stargazing.

As an astrogeologist, Owl was particularly excited to accompany the girls on a crick stomp. They were soon distracted picking up rocks, but I stuck by Owl and let my curiosity show.

"Look here," she said, pointing to a place on a gravel bar where flattish rocks were stacked up against each other like shingles. "When we see rocks like this, we know that water once flowed there." "*Obviously*," I thought in my teenage head, "*this is a creek*." Owl continued, "By learning about rocks on Earth, we can also learn more about rocks on other planets. If we see rounded rocks or rocks stacked up like this on other planets, we know that there was once water flowing there also." "*Hmmm . . .*" I thought, and tucked that bit of knowledge away in my brain.

As I went on to take geology courses in college, Owl's words snuck back into my consciousness time and again. In class we learned about reading the story of ancient streams in the structure of the bedrock they had become. Knowing this gave me new eyes for observing flowing streams and the rocks they move.

In the summer of 2012 I was barely aware of NASA's latest project —the Mars rover "Curiosity"—until a geologist friend posted a news article on Facebook. The headline read: "NASA's Curiosity Finds Water Once Flowed on Mars." The detailed photos showed rounded pebbles and streambed characteristics that could only have been formed by running water.

Scientists gathered enough data to estimate that the stream was between ankle and hip deep and flowed about three feet per second. The characteristics of this Martian stream are preserved in a conglomerate, the type of rock formed when pebbles and sand become cemented together.

Reading NASA's report, I was immediately transported back to crick stomping with Owl in our shallow stream. "By learning about rocks on Earth," she had said, "we can also learn more about rocks on other planets . . . we can know that there was once water flowing there also." Thanks to Owl, and a little Curiosity, the alien landscape of Mars seems a lot more familiar.

When I met Owl, finding evidence of surface water on Mars was a lofty goal for the future of space exploration. Now that the future is here, I wonder what the next generation of space exploration will look like, and if any of those crick-stomping girls will join the adventure.

The Magic of Nature

Victoria Zalatoris

Gray mist hung in the air over Lake Namakagon, and clouds diffused the early morning sunlight. Fall colors seem deeper and richer in wet weather and half-light like this. As I turned up County Highway D, I was dismayed to find it converted to dirt, with bright orange Road Work Ahead signs adding their own garish color to the landscape. I was a little irritated that crunchy gravel, washboards, and heavy machinery would interrupt my scenic drive.

At first I traveled at about my normal speed, since the curves and scenery of this winding road encourage slow driving anyway. Then I reached the flagger with the stop sign showing. After a moment of irritation, I noticed a movement out of the corner of my eye. Something small, white, and furry sat quivering in the roadside grass. It scurried a few steps, then froze and looked alert on its haunches. From nose to bushy white tail, the critter was only about eight inches long—the size of a least chipmunk.

Least chipmunks are the smallest and most widely distributed North American chipmunk, focusing their range in the north and west. Their larger cousins, the eastern chipmunks, range throughout Wisconsin and the eastern United States. Both are usually light brown with dark brown and white stripes, live in burrows in a variety of habitats, feed primarily on seeds, and spend the winter underground sleeping and eating occasionally. They do not need special camouflage to blend in with the snow like snowshoe hares, so why was this one white?

Two different genetic conditions result in pale animals. The most familiar is albinism. In albino animals, two recessive genes combine and result in the loss of the animal's ability to produce an important brown pigment called melanin. Melanin protects us from ultraviolet light and increases as we get our summer suntan.

Without melanin all parts of the animal are white or pink. The pink color, as in the eyes of a true albino, is a result of blood vessels showing through. Melanin is necessary for sight and for eye development, and albino humans, as well as animals, often have impaired vision.

Another genetic condition results in animals with pale fur but normal eyes, or patches of white or washed-out colors. These critters are leucistic. Birdwatchers regularly report seeing leucistic robins and other birds with oddly pale feathers.

In contrast, some animals produce far more melanin than usual. These melanistic animals are dark brown or black. Some neighborhoods boast about having a high number of black squirrels. These are simply melanistic gray squirrels. In contrast to albinism, melanism is often helpful to an animal for camouflage, and in the case of black leopards, it also gives them disease resistance.

People often attribute mystical or spiritual significance to albino animals. In University of Texas tradition, seeing an albino squirrel before an exam confers good luck. In Ojibwe tradition, albino bucks represent the sacredness of all living things, and seeing one should remind us to contemplate our own spirituality.

I could not tell for sure which the scurrying chipmunk was—albino or leucistic—but I knew I had to try to get a photo. I fumbled for my camera, rolled down the window, turned off the engine, and snapped a few shots. Before long, a gentle breeze carrying the sweet scent of autumn leaves wafted through the window and past my nose. I took a deep breath and looked out at the sparkling water of Lake Namakagon. With the radio and engine off, my hurried brain quieted, too. This little white critter transformed road construction from an inconvenience into a moment of peace. Ah, the magic of nature.

Flights of Yellow

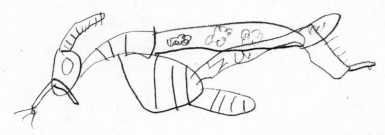

Norah Werner, age 5

Yellow wings flash and click knee-high next to my bike. Up ahead, several sets of yellow wings flap quickly up to the trees. A gentle breeze releases yellow sugar maple leaves from their twigs, and they flutter gracefully to the ground. This sunny gravel road glimmers with the yellows of late summer.

The first yellow wings belong to the Carolina grasshopper. While not especially numerous, they are probably the most common grasshopper we see. They prefer roadsides, weedy lots, and yards, and their yellow bands along the edge of black hind wings do a great job of catching our attention.

The grasshoppers' yellow wing bands flash briefly as they make short flights to escape from predators (or us). When flushed, they fly at a right angle to the predator's line of travel, then hunker down and use their mottled brown body and forewings to disappear.

To find food, Carolina grasshoppers make lazy, bobbing

flights about two feet off the ground, and are often mistaken for butterflies. To find mates, males rise almost vertically from the ground to heights of three to six feet, occasionally higher, and hover for eight to fifteen seconds. Then they flutter down near where they started. Late summer is their mating season, and the eggs will hatch next June.

Males, and sometimes females, produce sound in flight. The snapping, crackling, or buzzing sound is made by rubbing the under surface of the forewings against the veins of the hind wings. The short flights attract both females and other males. They remind me of frogs calling each other into a vernal pool in the spring or prairie chickens displaying on a booming ground.

The second group of yellow wings belongs to yellow-shafted northern flickers. As the migrating flock spooks off down the road in front of me, handsome yellow feathers flash from under their wings and tails, and yellow feather shafts show through from above and below. Their white rump patches glint brightly and give another vibrant identification clue.

These woodpeckers spend most of their time feeding on the ground, where their smooth brown backs with black bars and dots blend in well with soil and leaf litter. They catch ants and other insects (but not grasshoppers!) with their long, sticky tongues, and dig up anthills to access tasty larvae. Ants are not just food, but also pest control. Flickers rub formic acid from the ants onto their feathers during preening to help prevent parasites.

When flushed, flickers make short, undulating flights up to low branches and often perch like robins instead of clinging to the trunk like most woodpeckers. Instead of the snapping sound of grasshoppers, the song of the northern flicker is a loud wick-wick-wick-wick or a squeaky flick-a, flick-a, often accompanied by a long continuous roll of drumming on spring mornings.

This time of year flickers head south. They are one of the only migratory woodpeckers. Soon harsh frosts will silence the grasshoppers, and maple leaves will have made their own journeys to the forest floor. The brilliant wings of fall are bringing beauty and change.

FALL

The Wings of a Dobsonfly

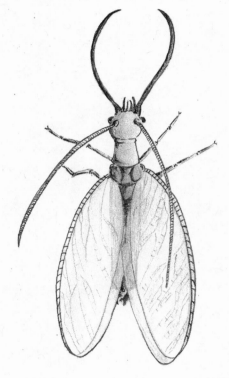

Leslie Strapon

Autumn is certainly pretty. Crimson leaves on the swamp maples shine through the fog, and the sweet smell of wet leaves rises from the forest floor. Bracken ferns and dogbanes glow yellow from the dry ditches, while up above them, birch and aspen leaves hang crinkled and brown. Here and there, a sugar maple reveals its hiding place with a flame of orange.

Of course the thing about all this beauty is that it precedes death and death-like dormancy. Past and current droughts can stress the plants and rush the fall color changes, but even in a perfect weather year the dying would come eventually. It's not just the plants, either.

The other evening, a giant insect buzzed against my lamplit screen. Imagine a dragonfly's ugly stepbrother. This dobsonfly had two pairs of clear wings with brown markings, a long, lumpy body, and huge mandibles (jaws). Dobsonflies spend two to three years in an aquatic larval stage, during which they are called "hellgrammites," "grampus," or "go-devils," by anglers who use them as bait.

The huge mandibles on this male dobsonfly are used exclusively to mate. Neither he nor she can eat, and each lives only seven days.

Dozens of other things also are dying this time of year. Soon bald-faced hornets will freeze to death in their papery nests. On my window frames, the exoskeletons of dark fishing spiders cling to their nursery webs, dried legs curled beneath them. Deer lay bloated along the highway, and more will soon hang in hunters' sheds.

But what is death in the natural world? That dobsonfly's body will be eaten by a bird or a fish or bacteria. His cells will be broken down into their chemical components, and his carbon will become bird or fish or soil or the air you are breathing. Sweet-smelling leaves are being decomposed by bacteria who feed a complex food web in soil. The deer's constituent parts will fly off as a crow or fuel a hunter's footsteps. The form changes, but life continues.

Even you are dying, a little bit at a time, and being recycled. Dead skin sloughs off as you sleep and is eaten by (ew!) dust mites in your pillow. Elements that were once part of your body—filling your lungs, flowing through your veins, and building the cells of your liver, spleen, bones, and hair—are passed back and forth between you and the world. Maybe that maple tree that you walked under today will have a little bit of you in it soon—just like your elements were once part of a photosynthesizing plant or that tomato you ate for lunch. I love being me, but how exciting to think about decomposing into the crimson leaves on a swamp maple, the wings of a dobsonfly, or a gust of wind.

As I sit here thinking about death on a beautiful autumn day, I take a deep breath of happiness. In nature death is part of life. This *is* the prettiest world, and we will forever continue to be part of its cycles.

Sharpies at Hawk Ridge

Mason McKay, age 10

"Hold it like an ice cream cone," instructed Gail
Johnejack, education director at Hawk Ridge Bird
Observatory, as she skillfully wrapped her hand around
mine and guided my fingers into a careful grip on feathers
and legs. When she transferred the bird into my care, I
could feel the heartbeat in my own skin. A breeze ruffled

the sharp-shinned hawk's feathers, and I imagined we were both eager for her to continue her long migration journey. Beyond the bird stretched the city of Duluth and the shimmering water of Lake Superior.

Hawk Ridge in Duluth, Minnesota, is one of the top five hawk migration sites in North America for overall numbers and diversity of species. Each fall about 82,000 raptors pass through this bottleneck on their southern migration. Understandably reluctant to cross a large body of water, the birds funnel southwest along the shore of Lake Superior. The high, rocky outcrop of Hawk Ridge Nature Reserve makes a great viewing platform, and people come together from all over the country to watch the migration.

It's not easy, though. The soaring travelers are often tiny specks against the blue. Raptor biologists at Hawk Ridge have a special trick for getting close-up views of the hawks—bait. Using a technique a lot like fishing, researchers pull the string on a lure to make it look like an injured bird. When a raptor swoops down for an easy meal, it becomes tangled in one of a series of nets. Researchers carefully extricate it from the net, take a variety of measurements, and attach a numbered band to its leg. "Our utmost priority is to keep the raptors safe," assured Gail. "When a raptor is captured for banding, it is held for a very short time, and then we let it get on its way."

About 3 percent of birds banded here are later recaptured. Based on the data collected from recapturing banded birds, sharp-shinned hawks migrating over Hawk Ridge generally head southeast to Illinois and then southwest toward eastern Texas and Mexico, following the prevailing wind pattern.

Sometimes Hawk Ridge naturalists bring a recent captive down from the remote banding station so that folks on the overlook can get a better view. Moments after we arrived, two naturalists called everyone over to see a couple of "sharpies" in hand. To prevent the hawks from hurting the humans or themselves, the naturalists held their wings, tail, and legs gently but firmly in the fist of one hand. The birds, both hatch-year females, looked quite calm.

Sharp-shinned hawks are the smallest hawks in North America and have the biggest size difference between males and females. Females are up to one-third larger than males, and this size difference means that they focus on different sizes of prey. Males tend to hunt smaller birds, such as sparrows, while females can concentrate on larger prey, like robins. This has two main advantages: males and females do not compete for the same food source, and chicks can get appropriately sized food as they grow.

During the first few weeks after hatching, the female sharp-shin broods the chicks while the male hunts and brings in small songbirds. He typically removes and eats the head before delivering the meal. As the chicks mature, the female joins in the hunting and brings larger prey for the hungry fledglings.

Sharp-shinned hawks are agile and acrobatic fliers, navigating dense woods at high speeds by using their long tail as a rudder. Short, rounded wings help them zip through tight spaces after small birds. During migration, they leave the dense forests of their northern nesting grounds and take to the open sky.

To help make the journey easier, these and other hawks will ride thermals, which are rising pockets of warmer air that are formed by the uneven heating of the surface of the Earth. Thunderheads are visible thermals, where clouds of water droplets show just how high the warm air is climbing. When turkey vultures or other birds are soaring in lazy circles without flapping, they are riding thermals.

For every mile a bird rises on this avian elevator, it can coast downwind seven miles without flapping. Still, sharp-shinned hawks' migration from the top of this continent to the bottom takes strength, endurance, and stored energy. To prepare for the journey, these small hawks grow furiously—going from egg to adult size in just over seven weeks.

I gripped the sharp-shinned hawk carefully, amazed at both her sturdiness in my hand and also the strength I could sense in her muscles. Erik Bruhnke, count interpreter, positioned himself just over the cliff, camera in hand. All day, Erik alternated between spotting and identifying birds, answering visitors' questions, and taking photos of hawk releases. He was a wealth of information.

"I've watched birds all my life, but I'm not a bird watcher," Harry, a Hawk Ridge volunteer, said humbly. "I'm just trying to become one! One of the benefits of Hawk Ridge is that amateurs can learn from all the real birders that are here." Erik was equally thrilled with the arrangement and said, "Teaching is the best way to learn. Working here really helps me learn about birds on a deeper level."

Harry is retired, like many Hawk Ridge volunteers. He enjoys interacting with the other main type of volunteer—college students fulfilling requirements for courses. Harry loves his job, because "volunteers and visitors both find commonality and community in the birds—they draw us all together as a group. It keeps me young!" Harry said.

The natural setting is also a bonus. Bright sunshine, a warm breeze, and a terrific view are a stunning combination. Even chilly, gray days have a certain beauty. Harry likes the full spectrum: "When we hawk watchers arrive on the first of September, we look down on the city in full summer green. By the time we leave on October 31, most of the leaves are gone. We are blessed with seeing the complete transition of fall."

And I'm thrilled to see this hawk transition back to her journey. "Now you're going to be the Statue of Liberty," Gail instructed. "Hold your arm up high. When Erik counts to three, give it a little toss into the air."

I raised my right arm high. It was thrilling to hold such an amazing creature for even a few seconds, and thrilling to be a part of its freedom. "One . . . two . . . three!" counted Erik. I released my grip with a gentle toss and watched in awe as the raptor took flight. She swooped down below the cliff and darted among trees before disappearing from sight. Close on her tail, three more hawks materialized out of the north and zipped past the eager crowd.

"It's hawk migration season!" exclaimed Gail. "We love helping people experience this great event!"

Long Live the Queen

Donna Post

There's something in the air this time of year. The sunshine is especially golden, red leaves are beginning to appear on the trees, and "mosquito hour" is reduced to "mosquito five minutes." It's easier than ever to spend quality time outside with loved ones. There is romance in the air as some species prepare for winter by finding a mate before they hibernate. Many insects do this, including bees and bald-faced hornets.

Bald-faced hornets *(Dolichovespula maculata)* are wasps who are three-quarters-of-an-inch long with

black-and-white markings. The queens are the only
ones who survive the winter, and fall is the time when
they prepare for hibernation. Newly hatched queens will
mate with a male drone, and then the mated females will
burrow into the ground or an old tree stump, or squeeze
behind a comfy flap of tree bark to wait for spring. All the
rest of the colony (male drones, female workers, and the
old queen) die of old age or freezing temperatures.

Late fall is a good time to find their abandoned nests,
long after all the nest defenders are gone. The nests are
as large as a basketball, shaped like a football, and usually
attached to a twig in a shrub or tree. If you cut open an
abandoned bald-faced hornet nest, you'll notice several
papery layers of insulation surrounding the hexagonal
chambers of the nursery combs. Paper wasps have similar
habits, but their nests are open, with no insulation
surrounding the combs.

Early next spring, in April or May, the new queens will
emerge from hibernation and begin the life cycle anew.
Each queen will make paper for her own nest by chewing
up wood fibers and mixing them with her sticky saliva.
The colony starts with just a few paper cells arranged in a
honeycomb-like structure attached to a twig. The queen
lays one fertilized egg in each six-sided cell, and once the
eggs hatch she feeds the larvae with a high-protein baby
food of chewed up insects. At some point, when the larvae
have had enough, they spin a white silk roof over their cell
and pupate. They later emerge as infertile female workers.

Once the queen raises the first generation of workers, they take over all the nest building and child-rearing duties, and she spends her time laying eggs. As adults, hornets don't grow because their exoskeleton is hard and fixed. They mostly eat sugary foods like nectar and rotten fruit for energy.

When workers are in the nest, they shiver to produce heat. Their warmth is retained by the layers of insulation. This allows the larvae to develop more quickly and the adults to maintain the 95 degree body temperate required for fast flight and nest defense. If you accidentally bump a nest in the summer, the thin paper shell will rip, and hundreds of hornets may fly out to sting you. They don't have barbs on their stingers, which allows them to each sting multiple times. This fierce defense is necessary because the larvae in the nest are tasty, protein-rich treats for birds, bears, foxes, skunks, and raccoons.

In late summer and early fall, the queen lays two different types of eggs. One set will be unfertilized eggs that hatch into male drones. Wasps, bees, and ants don't have X and Y chromosomes to determine sex like humans do. Instead, females hatch from fertilized eggs and are diploid (having two sets of chromosomes like humans), and males hatch from unfertilized eggs, so are haploid (having only one set of chromosomes).

The final round of larvae from fertilized eggs pupates into fertile female adults with more fat stores and chemicals to protect them against freezing damage—these are the new queens. They mate with a drone and then hibernate until the next spring when the cycle begins again.

Spring and fall are the seasons when we are reminded over and over of all the cycles present in nature. As the heat subsides, the humidity falls, and the kids go back to school, take a deep breath and appreciate the beauty of the season.

Why Wisconsin Forests Look the Way They Do

Kaia Neal, age 13

Sunlight filtered through the maple and aspen leaves as we gathered on the narrow, dirt trail. John Kotar, emeritus professor of forest ecology from UW–Madison, gestured widely as he described tree species, shade tolerance, soil moisture, and glacial history. With the title "Why Wisconsin Forests Look the Way They Do," John's field trip aspired to summarize his life's research in just a few hours.

Several years ago, John developed an ecological classification system for Great Lakes forests, and he published *A Guide to Forest Communities and Habitat Types of Northern Wisconsin*. His in-depth knowledge of our forests meant that wherever we stopped along the trail, he had something to say.

"I've been trying to think of a good analogy for the way I see the forest versus how a regular person sees it," he said. "Imagine that you enter a room filled with people you don't know. There is a wide mix of ages, appearances, etc. You just see people. Few details would stick out, and you might not be able to derive any information from the assemblage. Now imagine walking into your family reunion. You scan the crowd and instantly know who everyone is, how they've changed over time, and how they relate to everyone else in the room. That's how I—that's how foresters—see the forest. Most people just see trees."

So we swatted mosquitoes and looked a little closer. A sugar maple, with its smooth leaf margins and U-shaped interlobes, stood tall near the trail. Its many children, stunted from shade but tough and long lasting, carpeted the opening as seedlings.

The presence of sugar maple indicates that this soil has a fair amount of moisture and nutrients. Soil moisture and nutrients are the two primary factors that John focused on to develop his classification system. On the ground, the small, leathery leaves of wintergreen quietly contradict the sugar maple. Wintergreen is an indicator of poorer soils.

The nature of this forest, and any natural community anywhere, is the result of multiple factors. John's two primary factors are intimately related to another set of factors often used by ecologists to understand the landscape: geologic history, recent disturbance, and current climate.

Just south of Lake Namakagon in northwest Wisconsin, the pertinent geologic history revolves around glaciers. The Superior and Chippewa lobes of the most recent Wisconsin glaciation stalled out here for a while, dumping tons of clay, silt, sand, pebbles, cobbles, and boulders into lumpy hills called moraines. This mix of sediment sizes moderates both the soil moisture and the soil nutrients, resulting in sugar maple and wintergreen growing together.

Behind us, a red maple with sharp, toothy leaves and a cluster of smaller trunks all sprouted from a cut stump reminded us of the most widespread recent disturbance— logging. The forest in this recreational area has been logged a few times since the initial cut in the late 1800s.

Dying paper birches on the edge of the opening also express the forest's memory of a sunnier time. As a pioneer species, paper birches need full sun to get established. Then as more shade-tolerant trees grow up around the birches, they surrender their place or hope for a fire. Shade-tolerant balsam firs form thickets in the understory and will rise to the top over time.

Our current climate, with adequate rainfall, cold winters, and hot summers plays an important role in determining which plants even have the option of living here. You won't find a cactus in this forest, and neither will you find a baobab tree. Microclimates affect the forest on a local scale: black ashes grow in low, wet spots while oaks might claim a dry, sunny hill.

In the crisp fall sunshine, we wandered down the trail. The forest changed gradually as we passed through an aspen grove, a balsam thicket, and more maples. Someone asked how these forests have changed over time. While white pines were the most commonly logged species at the turn of the century, they weren't necessarily a bigger part of the forest. Their ability to float on rivers to reach sawmills was their downfall.

Today white pines tower above their neighbors on almost every soil type in Wisconsin. While we (both we on this hike and we as ecologists) started off by describing which trees do best where, scientists are always trying to look deeper and ask "why?" or "how?"

Sometimes it is not just about one species, but how several work together. In 2001 soil ecologists discovered that white pine and other trees get some of their nitrogen from tiny soil arthropods called springtails. But first, a fungus—the bicolored deceiver (*Laccaria bicolor*)—must kill and decompose the springtail using special enzymes. Then the fungus forms a sheath around the roots of the white pine and transfers the nitrogen and other nutrients to the tree in exchange for sugars produced during photosynthesis. About 95 percent of plants get similar supplemental nutrition from fungi.

Even small variations in the look of our forests, like the extra-vibrant fall colors in swamps, have explanations if we ask the right questions. In 2003 a grad student found that in places where the soil was lower in nitrogen and other important elements (such as swamps), red maple trees produced more of the red pigment anthocyanin in their leaves. This sunscreen pigment allows the tree to recover more nutrients from their leaves before they fall.

I love looking at a forest on the broad scale and thinking about the giant chunk of ice that shaped my home. I also love finding out about these detailed and cryptic connections. Nonetheless, you don't have to delve into the science to enjoy the fact that Wisconsin forests, especially in autumn, look the way they do.

The Forest Rainbow

Mason McKay, age 10

Sunlight streamed through a golden canopy of maple and poplar leaves, bathing the hiking trail in warm energy. The group chatted merrily, their lively conversations keeping pace with eager hiking boots and bright moods reflected in bright clothes. Pink and purple leaves on the maple-leaf viburnum added color to the understory, while the last remaining berries on bluebead lily and blue cohosh stalks provided accents. The fall forest was a rainbow of color.

But not all the most interesting colors were immediately apparent. As my boot scuffed the dry, brown leaves on the side of the trail, a glimpse of vivid color caught my eye. Buried beneath the fading leaf litter was a bright red fungus. As I brushed the crinkly leaves aside, my fingertips relished the smooth, slippery texture of the mushroom's cap.

Aptly named the scarlet waxy cap, clusters of this beautiful mushroom have been livening up my hikes lately. Their particular shade of red, with yellow on the margin of the cap, can hide perfectly among freshly fallen maple leaves, but stands out jauntily against green moss or brown birch leaves.

Since this mushroom is easy to identify, it is tempting to harvest it for my kitchen. It is reported as "mild tasting" and is eaten throughout its habitat in Europe and Asia. However, since some mycophagists (people who eat mushrooms) in North America have reported adverse reactions to the scarlet waxy cap, I have decided to enjoy it solely in the woods.

After examining that first patch of waxy caps, I began to see them peeking up among leaves all along the trail. Then I started seeing fungi everywhere! Lichens (composed of fungus and algae) encrusted all the trees, shelf fungi gave trunks interesting silhouettes, and rows of turkey tail mushrooms lined every fallen log.

Turkey tails are some of most common mushrooms found on wood in the world. They are a type of bracket fungi, meaning that they form thin, leather-like and leaf-like structures in concentric circles. When you flip a scarlet waxy cap upside down, you find rows of bright yellow gills. On the underside of a turkey tail, you find tiny pores.

It is the upper surface of a turkey tail mushroom that provides its name. Concentric rings of brown, orange, maroon, blue, and green remind us of the iridescent tail feathers on a wild turkey. While not as bright as the waxy cap, the turkey tail has a subtle beauty and is worth close examination. It also has medical uses.

Turkey tail mushrooms have been used to treat various maladies for hundreds of years in Asia, Europe, and by indigenous peoples in North America. Traditionally, our ancestors boiled mushrooms in water to make a soothing tea. Records of turkey tail brewed as medicinal tea date from the early fifteenth century during the Ming Dynasty in China. A few years ago, my Aunt Nan used turkey tail tea to boost her immune system during a battle with cancer, and she outlived the doctor's predictions by several years. Last summer, a promising clinical study showed that the turkey tail mushroom (*Trametes versicolor*) improves the immune systems of breast cancer patients.

As I examined a log covered with little bracket fungi, I noticed that some of them looked purple around the margin instead of the typical white. When I broke one off to examine it more closely, I found a very different mushroom!

The plain white cap of a violet-toothed polypore hides a gorgeous lavender secret. If you flip one over and tilt it, the color becomes almost iridescent as light bounces around the brightly colored pores. Though not medicinal, this mushroom always makes me smile. I can't wait to bring my young niece Kylee mushroom hunting, so she can look for her favorite color on every fallen log.

What she won't see as easily is the true body of the fungus. Scarlet waxy caps, turkey tails, and violet toothed polypores are saprophytic fungi, meaning that they decompose wood to obtain nutrients. The visible part of the mushroom is simply the reproductive structure, tasked with releasing spores. A network of fungal cells (called mycelia) penetrates the wood and does the actual decomposing. One analogy is that the mushroom is like an apple, with the mycelium like the tree.

You can sometimes find a web of black or white mycelia under the bark of a tree, beneath a rotting log, or under thick leaf litter. By some accounts, the world's largest known organism is an interconnected web of genetically identical mycelia in Oregon's Blue Mountains. This honey mushroom occupies 3.7 square miles of soils and could be as ancient as 8,650 years old.

All those mycelia are important links in the food chain since they play an enormous role in recycling nutrients from old plants and animals into new plants and animals. Can you imagine a forest without fungi? In the absence of wildfire (another decomposer), dead trees and plant debris would pile up, and new trees would not have enough nutrients to grow.

As our hike ended, the chatter continued right on into the cars. What fun it was to take a closer look at all the components in the forest's rainbow on a beautiful fall day!

Color: It's More Than Just Pretty

chlorophyll B

Heather Edvenson

Biking along Highway M on my way to work, I am dazzled by the gorgeous rainbow of color. It started with the red maples in the swamps. They turned scarlet several weeks ago, brightening up the landscape like nothing else can. The interrupted ferns and bracken ferns in the ditches turned yellow, and then a rapid cascade of other plants changed into their fall wardrobes. Now the forest is mostly orange and gold—from the thick litter of leaves on the ground all the way up to the crowns of the trees. During gloomier falls I often quip that this is the season when the sun shines from the ground *up*. Recently we've been surrounded by sunshine, with not a cloud in the sky.

While the colors this fall have been stunning, I like to think about how *useful* the colors are, too. Green plants, for example, get their color from chlorophyll, the powerhouse of photosynthesis. Chlorophyll captures the energy of the Sun, uses it to make sugar out of water and carbon dioxide, and supports the entire food chain—including us. We have all known this since grade school science class, but it never ceases to amaze me.

The yellows and oranges finally revealed during the past couple weeks were always there. They were just masked by the greater amount of chlorophyll. When the plant stops producing new chlorophyll, the old is broken down, and the other colors shine through. Yellow and orange aren't just useless underdogs—they have important jobs to do, too.

Yellow-colored xanthophylls are found in most plants, and they help keep the machinery of photosynthesis from being damaged by absorbing too much light. Animals get xanthophylls from their food, and we can see them in the color of egg yolks, butter, fat, skin, and even the macula lutea—a yellow spot in our retina where the pigment absorbs ultraviolet light to help protect our eyes.

Orange carotenoids (as in carrots) also absorb extra ultraviolet light. In addition they are antioxidants that capture renegade oxygen molecules. They support human health in the form of vitamin A.

Red anthocyanins aren't revealed in the same way that yellow and orange are. They are created from the breakdown of sugars once phosphate has been drawn from the leaf back down into the twigs. Sunlight is necessary to create anthocyanins (and more anthocyanins are needed in sunny weather), which is why sunnier autumns have more brilliant colors. We see red again in the new leaves of spring. During both seasons, the pigment protects against damaging light at low temperatures.

Anthocyanins protect humans, too, and have been shown to help stave off cancer, inflammation, diabetes, and bacterial infections. One study even showed that anthocyanins cause cancer cells to die faster! We don't eat red maple leaves for our health of course, but we do eat blackberries, blueberries, cranberries, and many other fruits with plenty of red in their skin and juice.

Speaking of red skin, kayaking on Lake Namakagon for three hours in the sun last week reminded me about the importance of melanin. This brown pigment not only protects humans, bacteria, and fungi from ultraviolet light (by creating our summer suntan), it is also important in the immune systems of invertebrates.

While I think the biochemistry of color is fascinating, there are many other ways that colors provide protection. As a gray-brown deer materializes from the shadows at dawn, camouflage comes to mind. In contrast, a bright-orange monarch butterfly fluttering by my paddle warns birds that it would be a bitter mouthful, simply through its vivid colors.

The pale, smooth trunk of a paper birch also has protective coloration—this time from heat. In winter, trees freeze very carefully to make sure that their cells are not damaged by ice. Darker trees may thaw and then freeze again too quickly, while pale, reflective birches stay cool and safe.

Paddling close to a loon, I was struck by the vibrancy of its red eyes. Even that color has a specific purpose. Under the water, red is the first light to be filtered out. Since we perceive color based on the wavelengths of light that are reflected off a surface, the loon's eye is reflecting red light and absorbing all others. This allows the loon's eyes to gather all possible light wavelengths while hunting in the depths.

My brown eyes are taking in as much as they can. Despite my love of science and explanations, I think one of the most wonderful uses of color is the rejuvenation of our hearts and souls in the presence of natural beauty.

Cedar Waxwings I:
The Death of Something Pretty

Laura Semken

The feathers are glossy brown and streaked with white. The tip of the tail looks like it was dipped in paint made from golden aspen leaves. A jet-black mask outlined by white extends from eyes forward to the nostrils. The warm body is limp and still. This beautiful young cedar waxwing died in my hands just now.

A moment ago as I rode up to the back of the Museum on my bike, exhilarated from the delicious air and golden morning sunlight, a loud thunk sounded from the window above my head. This lovely creature dropped at my feet. I observed it for a second to see if it would rouse on its own. It lay still, beak open, so I stooped to pick it up. As I held it, the beak opened and closed one last time. The lower eyelid slid up to cover a shiny, black eye, and the body slowly cooled.

While saddened by this death, I am thankful for an opportunity to examine such a beautiful bird up close. I often admire the adult cedar waxwings in our Museum collection, with their lovely yellow tail tips, rakish black masks, silky lemon breasts, and scarlet wax droplets on the wing feathers, but this one in my hand is different. Many birds change their plumage for the breeding season and then again for winter. Goldfinches are one of the most common and distinctive examples of this. Cedar waxwings, on the other hand, look the same all year round, and even males and females look virtually identical. Only immature cedar waxwings during their very first summer and fall look any different.

One of the purposes of museum collections is to represent and preserve the diversity of nature. Larger museums may have dozens of specimens of the same species representing various ages, sexes, seasons, and habitats. These can be used for research and study. While our tiny museum doesn't have the space to collect quite so extensively, we use our array of specimens to help visitors with identification and to illustrate concepts.

Although we already have two adult cedar waxwings preserved in our collection, this immature bird will be labeled with the date and location of its death and stored in our salvage freezer. This winter, a volunteer may mount it or preserve it as a study skin.

While the Museum has the capacity (and the state and federal permits) to salvage dead animals for educational purposes, we still feel saddened and shamed that our windows cause so many deaths. Millions of birds each year die in collisions with windows. Windows reflect the trees, and birds try to fly right through them. Some are just stunned, and if you hold them for a minute they may soon fly away. Others, like my cedar waxwing, suffer brain trauma or break their neck.

There are several things you can try to keep birds from hitting your windows. Window clings and silhouettes are somewhat effective, although you may need to attach them to the outside of the glass. Dangling things in front of windows can also help. We have pretty feather-shaped windsocks on our lower windows, but the not upper ones. We've recently started taping lengths of curling onto the windows as well. Mirrors, glass beads, old compact disks, and other pretty trinkets can be hung in front of windows to sway in the breeze. These moving objects tend to scare the birds away. Fine mesh netting can be stretched outside windows. This both reduces the reflection and softens the impact.

If a bird dies in a collision with your window, and it is fresh and in good shape, you can call and ask us (or another museum or nature center) if we need it for our collection. Then seal it in a plastic baggie in your freezer until you can bring it to the Museum. As long as you contact us, you will be covered under our permits until we make the transfer. While the death of something wild and beautiful is always sad, knowing that it can be used to teach hundreds of people about nature and conservation makes it just a little less tragic.

Cedar Waxwings II:
The Ecology of Beauty

Diana Randolph

As I wrote about the cedar waxwing that died a collision with a window, the rest of the flock chattered and whistled their high-pitched calls in the black cherry trees above me. This week the trees are silent and bare. Did our windows kill them all? No, thank goodness. It's natural for cedar waxwings to be an exciting presence one day and gone the next. These large, gregarious flocks are facultative migrants—they move around as their food supply requires. One day several dozen may descend on your bushes. The next day the shrubs will be empty of both birds and fruit. These songbirds dine heavily on many kinds of berries and also the tiny cones of eastern redcedar trees, hence their name.

As a kid in Iowa, I remember late winter days when colorful flocks of waxwings gathered in the highbush cranberry hedge (*Viburnum trilobum*) outside our kitchen window. The tart berries with a high acid content last well through the winter and provide a much-needed food source when less-hardy berries have dried out or spoiled. How fun it was to watch them pass berries bird to bird down a row if the cluster of fruit could only be reached by one at a time! The birds' beautiful feathers captured my mom's heart, too.

Since cedar waxwings prefer edge habitats like fields and riverbanks, they have adapted well to human-altered landscapes. Their population is stable or even increasing despite the heightened dangers of windows and cats in suburban settings. Brown-headed cowbirds share some habitat preferences with waxwings and are also doing well in fragmented, edgy habitats. The problem is that cowbirds are nest parasites who lay their eggs in the nests of other species and force other birds to raise their young.

The cowbird chicks grow fast and usually smother or push the host nestlings out of the nest. Cedar waxwings have a simple solution: they eat so few insects that brown-headed cowbirds in waxwing nests die from a lack of protein. (Although waxwings can go through stretches of strict vegetarianism, they are also skillful flycatchers. While paddling various rivers, I've admired their aerial acrobatics as they feasted on summer's abundance of insects.)

Eating berries has other benefits and consequences. Overripe fruit may ferment, causing waxwings to become intoxicated or even die if they overdose. Perhaps the bird who crashed into our window last week was a bit tipsy. A more benign outcome of being a frugivore is that the waxwing's tail tip, which is usually yellow, may become orange if it eats the berries of Morrow's honeysuckle, an introduced species, while the feathers are growing. The pigment rhodoxanthin (a red carotenoid pigment) is responsible for the color change.

As the birds fluttered between clusters of chokecherries, I caught glimpses of their bright red waxwings. Used to attract mates, the red markings are flattened extensions of feather shafts colored with a carotenoid pigment—similar to the pigments in carrots and autumn maple leaves. The waxwings obtain the color by modifying pigments acquired from their diet, and the color increases with age. These birds maximize their nesting success by mating with other birds of similar age and experience levels—information gathered at least partially by observing the number of red wax tips. This is one more example of why color is not just pretty!

Where is that gregarious flock now? Are they eating *your* chokecherries? Have they started in on the mountain ash berries and crabapples already? Watch for these year-round residents to visit a yard (and hopefully *not* a window) near you!

Green Islands

Ayla Baussan, age 6

Leaves fell like glitter on the sun-showered path. These tiny, yellow hearts of quaking aspen fluttered wildly as they descended, eventually ending up in drifts built upon the wilted bodies of their companions. Placid raindrops beaded up on their slick surfaces, shining like jewels in the slanting rays of afternoon sun. A gentle sweetness wafted on the lukewarm breeze.

I do love fall.

And yet I already miss (just a little) the vibrancy of a buzzing summer day. Maybe if we could hold on to that green energy for just a little longer . . .

The golden leaves almost all had their own little hitchhiker hiding out between those slick, waterproof leaf skins. My evidence? Bright green trapezoids of chlorophyll captured between the first and second veins on one side of the leaves' midribs. The trees are not responsible for the variegated leaves.

A small, brown moth with white-fringed wings laid an egg on the leaf petiole (stem) back in July. By September a translucent larva hatched and bored into the petiole causing the stem to swell a bit into a small gall. Munching its way up inside the leaf under the cover of darkness, the larva interrupted the mechanisms the tree normally uses to draw chlorophyll out of the leaf during the waning days of autumn. The result is a "green island" in the yellow aspen leaves (and a forest carpeted in Green Bay Packers colors).

Such a tiny caterpillar would dry out in the summer heat or if it tried to pupate high in the tree canopy. Instead, it takes advantage of pleasant fall weather and then hitchhikes on the falling leaf down to the damp forest floor. Once there, it steals a few more bites of the green energy it preserved and then pupates in relative safety and an agreeable microclimate. The soon-to-be-moth spends the winter in its cocoon, which is loosely woven to the surface of the now-brown leaf.

The receding snow and warming sun of May stimulate metamorphosis, and the new moth emerges from its winter sleep.

While apparently unstudied in the United States, this drab moth and its tiny caterpillar have a holarctic distribution. This means that they live across all the continents in the Northern Hemisphere. In fact, some of the information I have presented here was translated from Swedish and Dutch by the magic of the Google Translator! I can track this organism throughout the world by the universal language of scientific names. *Ectoedemia argyropeza* may not roll off your tongue, but scientists all over the planet use this one name to refer this particular species.

Whatever you call it, the vibrant green islands those moth larvae preserve are a lovely part of fall.

Treasures of the Secret Bog

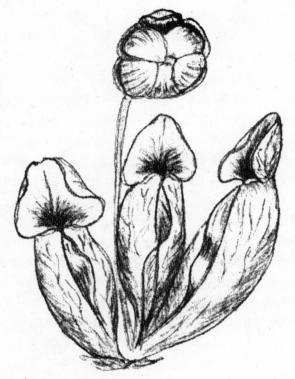

Lois Nestel

As a young girl, I loved the book *The Secret Garden*. I wished for a secret place all my own, where I could watch things grow and change. At that time, roses and other cultivated flowers seemed romantic. These days, I much prefer native wild plants to ornamental roses. Instead of a secret garden, I frequent a secret bog! Tucked away down a century-old logging road, to get to this bog I must push through thickets of balsam fir and climb through tangles of birch and aspen deadfalls. I brave ticks, wipe spider webs off my face, and get my feet wet. The treasures I find are worth every stick in my eye.

Last weekend was my first visit to the bog in a few months. Gone were the spring peepers and wood frogs, gone were the slender, green leaves of fen sedge, gone were the mosquitoes and black flies! Present were the tamaracks with their golden glow, the fluffy Truffula Tree-like seeds of cotton grass, and the gracefully twisted seedpods of blue flag iris.

Bogs are unique natural communities. In Wisconsin they have been developing for 10,000 years in sandy bowls left by the glaciers. The depressions were created when huge chunks of ice broke off from the main glacier and were buried in sand and gravel by the streams draining the melting ice mass. The sediment insulated the ice for a while, but it continued to melt slowly, eventually leaving a low area where the ice had been. Geologists call these glacial kettles. The high mounds of sand and gravel around them are known as kames. It's this process that helped create the rolling topography we love to ski and mountain bike on around the Cable area!

The unique history of these kettles has a big impact on the hydrology of bogs, or the way that water flows in and out of them. It doesn't. True bogs don't have inlets or outlets and are perched high above groundwater influence. All of their water comes from rain and snow. Rain and snow are both slightly acidic, and as dead leaves soak in the water, more acids are released. The process is very similar to steeping your morning cup of tea. (In fact, several bog plants make delicious tea!) Without flowing water, there is little oxygen. Organic matter decays slowly or not at all, forming black, organic soil called peat. Sphagnum moss, leatherleaf, and many other plants build up a thick mat of vegetation until the bog is almost dry. Sometimes the mat quivers like a waterbed and hides open water underneath.

Limited nutrients and oxygen do reach the margins of the bog through rainwater runoff. This causes a narrow band with higher decomposition rates, allowing open water to form in a ring around the bog. Last May, the moat was deep and squishy, and a class of seventh graders almost didn't make it across (due to squeamishness, not danger). Now the moat is mostly solid and grassy.

As I stepped out into the golden-brown heath, my mission was to find treasure. Not silver or diamonds—they aren't very flavorful. I was seeking cranberries. Displayed attractively on emerald mosses, the ruby-red fruits did look like jewels. I scoured each hummock for fruit: sometimes finding none, sometimes one, sometimes a dozen. With back bent, I nosed onto the next mound of moss and twigs. The high places around small tamarack trees seemed to be productive. I found one cluster of berries tangled in a dried thatch of grass. Some of the little globes were fermented and burst in my fingers. Others, buried so deep in moss they hadn't frozen, were still only pale cream with red speckles.

The picking went slowly. This was partly because the cranberries were few and hidden, but mostly because I was distracted by the other treasures. In one flat, mossy patch there were a dozen dried flower spikes, each about six inches high. Dry weed identification is a fun challenge, so I poked around their bases looking for clues. I found a tiny cluster of leaves. Curled tightly like fiddlehead ferns, they could only be the hibernaculum of a sundew. Sundews are carnivorous plants, well adapted to the nutrient-poor habitat in bogs. In summer tiny drops of "dew" glisten on the tips of hairs that cover small spoon-shaped leaves. The sticky mucilage "dew" traps insects and then digests them. Essential nutrients (especially nitrogen) are absorbed through the leaves. Just like trees have prepared for next year by forming leaf buds that will weather the winter, these sundews are ready and waiting for next spring.

Pitcher plants, another carnivorous plant in our bog, have also shut down for winter. I split open one bright-red leaf (they also change colors for fall, just like trees) and found a "bug-sicle" inside. The insects caught in the sweet-smelling digestive juices of the pitcher-shaped leaf will have to wait until next spring to be digested. Ice filled every leaf in the cluster of plants.

After about two hours of searching, I had one quart of

cranberries and two cold feet. Back at home, I warmed up quickly as a cake baked and the cranberries simmered with honey and cinnamon. That was the initial goal of my expedition: chocolate cake with cranberry sauce. I could have just gone to the grocery store, but I found so much more than fruit in my secret bog.

The Weird Ones

Charlie Hohn

The scent of snow fills the air, and the hissing plops of wet snow dropping off the trees fill my ears. The woods and its inhabitants are transitioning between fall and winter. It's the same for me as I jog down the road in my summer hat and winter gloves, yearning for ski season to arrive.

Early fall was a time of vibrant colors and a flurry action. Colors have faded a bit now. I've come to appreciate the subtle gold of a tamarack swamp and the rich browns in an oak grove as they extend the fall color season. But have you ever stopped to think about how weird those two trees are?

Tamaracks are conifers, bearing their seeds in cones just like their relatives the pines, spruces, and firs. But conifer isn't our first-choice word for describing pines—we'd rather call them evergreens. When we do that, though, tamarack doesn't fit. It is the only deciduous (losing its leaves seasonally) conifer in the Northwoods. Oaks, in contrast, are in a group known as broad-leaf trees, most of whom are deciduous. Yet oaks cling to their leaves.

Why would a tamarack lose its needles? Why would a pine keep its needles? And why does the oak keep its dead leaves?

There is adaptive value in each strategy; otherwise they would not persist. Needles are just modified leaves, better suited to low nutrient, low moisture situations. They have most of the same parts as a maple leaf, but everything is more tightly packed and protected. The stomata (pores for gas exchange) hide in a groove, protected from dry winds. A waxy outer layer helps to prevent water loss. By retaining green, chlorophyll-filled leaves all year, evergreen trees can take advantage of warm days to photosynthesize and save themselves the trouble and nutrient expense of growing new leaves each spring. They replace only about a third of their needles per year.

On the other hand, broad-leafed deciduous trees—like maples—grow large leaves with a lot of surface area for photosynthesis. The broad leaves also result in a lot of water loss. This is fine when it is raining, but not when the ground is frozen. Although trees use enzymes to protect their leaves from freezing while they are still photosynthesizing, that only works for so long. Then, frost-damaged leaves would become a liability as an entrance for disease.

Why would tamaracks combine the two strategies and lose their needles? Well, we don't know for sure, but my favorite theory is that it has something to do with how far north the tamarack's range extends. On the winter solstice, Duluth, Minnesota, will only have 8 hours and 32 minutes of sunlight. In Fairbanks, Alaska, near the northern edge of the tamarack's range, the sun will shine weakly for 3 hours and 42 minutes. Most of the tamarack's habitat is in the middle of that range. What good are green needles if there is little sunshine? By building more delicate needles that don't have to withstand harsh winter conditions, tamaracks can save a little energy.

In contrast, what good are the dead, brown leaves of an oak, even with sunshine? Oaks are broad-leaf trees, but they hang onto their leaves until heavy snow knocks them off or until new leaves push them out. Most deciduous trees (including tamaracks) disconnect their leaves by growing a protective abscission layer on the end of the twig, encouraging the leaf to skedaddle with digestive enzymes or a new layer of cells.

In contrast, oak leaves start to grow an abscission layer

soon after new buds form, but they do not finish the process until the next spring. Scientists call this retention of dead stuff "marcescence."

Plant physiologists agree that marcescence is a juvenile trait, associated with young trees and newer branches. This makes sense, since the young aspens in the field near my house are still holding onto their leaves. Likewise, understory trees, which tend to be younger, always seem to change colors later in the fall.

Marcescence may also be juvenile in terms of evolutionary history. In southern regions some oaks are evergreen. Our northern oaks may be in transition from being fully evergreen to being fully deciduous. Maybe they are not done yet—or maybe they like where they've paused!

Although tasty new buds are preparing to emerge in the spring, this year's dead, dry, crinkly oak leaves are not very palatable, and that may deter deer and moose from nibbling on the new growth. The tardily deciduous aspens—with their buds right at teeth height—may gain that benefit, too.

Another hypothesis is that the oaks are saving their leaves until spring. When the leaves fall, they will provide the tree with nutrient-rich mulch just in time for the growing season, instead of the leaves decomposing throughout the winter. Leaves dangling from lower branches may also act as a snow fence, trapping extra moisture for the tree.

There is no way for us to know for sure just what the oak is "thinking" as it rustles its skirt of leaves in the middle of a blizzard. Nor can we understand what the tamarack is "planning" when it waves a golden flourish and then bares its knobby twigs for the winter.

As with humans, the weirdest organisms are often the most interesting. At least that's what I hope, since some of you probably think I'm weird for wanting ski season to start in October!

Fairies and Fuzz-butts

Deb Nelson

Do you believe in fairies?

I inhaled a few as I walked down to the lake on a warm, damp afternoon not long ago. Tiny, fluffy, bluish-white wisps floated in the fading sunlight. Like a swarm of gnats, only slower and more ethereal, the air was filled with fairies. I didn't gain any magical powers when one got sucked up my nose, but my curiosity was piqued.

My first encounter with these tiny creatures was while scooping up a pot of water for supper in the Boundary

Waters of northern Minnesota. My paddling partner, a more experienced USFS wilderness ranger, called the flying insects "fuzz-butts." Who was I to argue?

Years later on a hike I found a whole colony of similar beings, covered in white fuzz and clinging to alder branches like lint on yoga pants. The group had several ants tending them busily. Someone in the hiking group produced a likely name: woolly alder aphids.

Like most aphids, woolly alder aphids suck plant juices from a host. The alder shrub harvests sunlight, water, and air; the aphids harvest the alder's sap; and then the ants harvest sugary honeydew secreted by the aphids. In return, ants provide the aphids with some protection from predators.

All the aphids in a colony are live-born, flightless female clones of their mother—until the days grow short. A single generation with females AND males occurs in the fall, flies away, mates, and lays eggs (one per female!) that will overwinter on maple trees. By flying to a new host before laying eggs, the parents give their offspring (all girls again) a fresh start in the spring. Winged generations, like the flock of fairies I just saw, occur in response to food shortages as well as shorter days. Once the maple leaves get too tough, for instance, a new winged generation relocates to alders until winter triggers their mating and exodus again.

The alternation of generations is quite effective. While the aphids are feeding on the same host as their mother, having her exact genes is useful since she is presumably well adapted to that habitat. During times of stress, though, using sex to mix genes and produce offspring with multiple combinations of traits will help the next generation adapt to changing environmental conditions.

Both flighted and flightless aphids cover themselves in a white, woolly covering made of wax, which looks like mold, plant seeds, or just a mouthful of fluff, and provides an excellent defense against predation. Inhaling just one was enough to make me hold my breath when walking back through the cloud of aphids. Whether or not you believe in fairies, they are uncomfortable to get up one's nose.

More Than Meets the Eye

Emily Stone

Gray, gray, gray. The gently rippled surface of the lake was gray in the early morning calm. Gray fog and gray clouds hung low over the gray trunks of the trees. Then a dark form materialized out by the buoy. Shifting slightly, the shape revealed the white throat of a loon glowing through the gloom. As I watched, the loon dipped its face into the water, peering into the depths below. What it saw I can't imagine, but its purposeful dive suggested fish by the submerged rock pile. The loon's sudden appearance and dive reminded me that there is more to this silent gray lake than meets the eye.

Chick-a-dee-dee-dees in the balsam fir tree next to me reeled my mind's eye back up from the depths of the lake. The flock from my bird feeders had followed me down to the lake for breakfast. I pulled a few sunflower seeds out of my pocket and extended my hand toward the birds.

With a whirr of wings, the first chickadee swooped from the fir tree and landed on my fingertips. Tiny toenails pricked my skin, and one shiny black eye looked up at me from a cocked head. We examined each other tentatively.

I always feel a thrill when such a fluffy ball of wildness lands on me. I love the chance to see chickadees up close. Their backs are not pure gray but tinged with warm beige around the neck that spills over onto their sides. The edge between black cap and white cheeks is not smooth but shows finely divided feathers. The base of the black throat patch where it grades into white belly feathers is even more irregular.

The frustrating part is that although this is my third winter feeding chickadees from my hand, I still can't tell them apart. I'm not even aided by markings that distinguish male and female birds. So I wonder, how do the chickadees know whom to romance in the spring?

We have long known that many birds can see ultraviolet light, but it took scientists a while to decide to test the ultraviolet reflectance of their feathers on a broad scale. In one study researchers analyzed 139 species of birds that we see as sexually monochromatic. In other words, they tested birds that humans cannot identify as male or female by their colors. More than 90 percent of birds in the study had ultraviolet-reflecting feathers and were sexually dichromatic from the avian perspective. Of course birds can tell each other apart!

My neighborhood chickadees are part of this pattern. If we could see in the ultraviolet spectrum, we would know that the males are brighter white and deeper black than females. Females prefer males with the sharpest contrast between white and black patches, which reinforces the trait in each generation. Males also have larger black areas, which we could potentially observe if we looked carefully. Interestingly, males with bigger black bibs tend to have more reproductive success.

After a quick dart forward to grab a seed, the chickadee on my hand whirred off to a branch in a flourish of gray. As other members of the flock flitted around in nearby trees, I marveled at my thoroughly human-centric view of the world and tried to imagine life with more colors in my vision. Just then, the loon reappeared through the mirrored surface of the lake. There is so much more to this world than what meets the eye.

A Dandelion Smile

Ayla Baussan, age 6

A chilly breeze whipped around my head. Even a pale sun peeking through racing clouds did not improve the temperature. Head down, I hurried toward the post office. Then a spot of color made me stop and smile. A single yellow dandelion and its star of vibrant, toothy leaves nestled into the snow-flattened grass.

I've always loved dandelions. They popped up every summer in the kingdom of make-believe that was my yard and created a sea of sunshine in the farmer's hayfield across the back fence. Every spring I still pick one of the hardy flowers to give to my mom for her late April birthday. Unless I've flattened it in a card to send through the mail, she sticks the dandelion in a little vase on the sill above the kitchen sink.

As a kid, I continued picking dandelions all summer long. I'd split the stems lengthwise and watch as they coiled into beautiful curlicues when dunked in cold water. I soaked the fuzzy blossoms in water and made "lemonade" that I never drank. I almost hyperventilated while trying to blow every parachuted seed off the stem to make a wish. And every T-shirt I owned was stained with little brown circles from the juicy stems.

Even today, despite my awareness that dandelions are invasive weeds, I can't help admiring their tenacity. And I'm not alone. Buddhist monk, Thich Nhat Hanh, shared this poem (written by an anonymous student) in his book *Peace Is Every Step.*

> I have lost my smile,
> but don't worry.
> The dandelion has it.[1]

I smile whenever I see those cheerful weeds. Sometimes I even brave their bitterness and eat young leaves in salads. Other folks swear by the sap as a remedy for warts or foot fungus. Turns out, dandelions may be more useful than I ever imagined!

The Kazakh dandelion (*Taraxacum kok-saghyz,* a relative

of the one in most yards) is an excellent source of natural rubber. The milky sap in the root is so high in latex that one field of dandelions produces as much latex as the same size plot of rubber trees. In addition, the quality of dandelion latex is exactly the same as latex from a rubber tree and can be substituted one for one in the rubber formulation. To top it off, dandelion latex does not seem to trigger allergic reactions.

Russians discovered this amazing species of dandelion in the early 1930s in Kazakhstan. They tried to develop it as a domestic source of rubber. During World War II, when the Japanese controlled the supplies of rubber from Southeast Asia, researchers in the United States, Germany, Sweden, and Spain all jumped on the dandelion-rubber bandwagon. In the United States alone, land grant universities in 40 states conducted research on this lowly plant.

Most research came to a halt after the war ended in 1945. Today, an Internet search for dandelion rubber reveals that at least three separate tire companies are partnering with research institutions to make this new source of rubber viable on a commercial scale. Continental is working with Germany's Fraunhofer Institute for Molecular Biology and Applied Ecology. Bridgestone is coordinating with the Program for Excellence in Natural Rubber Alternatives at Ohio State University. Multinational tire manufacturer, Apollo Vredestein, also thinks dandelion rubber has potential and is collaborating on the project with KeyGene.

Despite the many benefits of dandelions—they grow like weeds on many soil types, reproduce like weeds with lots of seeds, and thrive in northern climates instead of subtropical forests—there are some obstacles, too. Dandelion juice transforms from a liquid to a solid on contact with the air, a process known as polymerization. This means that processors must use turpentine to chemically extract the latex from dandelion roots.

To eliminate the enzyme responsible for polymerization, German scientists at the Fraunhofer Institute have engineered a special virus. According to a *Discovery News* article, "Once inside, the virus deleted the offending genetic sequence from the Russian dandelion's DNA. Pop the head off an infected dandelion, and the latex begins to flow freely."[2] (Watch out, Mom! My shirts will have more than just little, brown, circular stains!)

It worked. But in Europe, creating transgenic dandelions is controversial. Now German researchers are using traditional selective breeding techniques to accomplish the same thing. At the same time, Continental is working with researchers to build the first-ever commercial-scale processing plant. (Hopefully they are also developing ways to make sure the superseeds don't escape into our yards!)

Maybe in the future, that field of dandelions across the back fence won't be full of weeds. It will be full of a cash crop, harvested by the same machines used to pull tulip bulbs. The sticky sap, once a stain on my favorite shirt, will help my airplane land safely in Germany so I can go for a ride in a car with dandelion tires. That would certainly make me smile.

"What is a weed? A plant whose virtues have never been discovered." —Ralph Waldo Emerson

Flight

Leah Trommer

I love things that help me get a new perspective on the world, so I always request a window seat. Taxiing to the runway, my face pressed to the scratched plastic window, I watched a flock of snow buntings swoop in unison above the grass. White flashed on their wings. There was grace in the unconsciousness of their flight.

Birds are so well adapted to travel through the air that their movements can seem effortless. Even when we notice how hard they are working, the power in an eagle's wings and the skill of a hummingbird's maneuvers fill us with a sense of awe. Human-designed flight was not so easy.

In the years since Icarus flapped his waxy wings toward the Sun in ancient Greek mythology (and fell into the ocean when they melted), humans haven't had much luck trying to copy birds. Paradoxically, the great success in human flight came when we stopped trying to mimic natural flyers and began designing from scratch, says Professor Spedding, chairman of the Department of Aerospace and Mechanical Engineering at the University of Southern California.

Here I was, ready to take to the air, casually fulfilling the dream of flight with millions of other people today. We turned down our runway and sped up. As the force pushed me back into the seat, I tried to imagine what it would be like to be a loon—running hard across the lake, splashing and pushing with broad feet, until finally achieving enough speed for liftoff. Even when I was no longer jostled by the bumps of Earth, I was still pressed back into my seat by the acceleration.

Loons have the heaviest wing loading of any flighted bird, so they, like airplanes, must gain speed in order to generate enough lift to leave the ground. They must maintain that speed, too, or risk a crash landing. Have you ever seen a loon fly slowly? Me neither. Like commercial airliners, loons need their wings mostly for long-distance trips and use wide-open spaces for takeoffs and landings.

This allows both planes and birds to survive with limited maneuverability.

I'm also fascinated to see a bird's-eye view of the landscape—to follow familiar rivers, highways, lakeshores, and forests while seeking to understand them from a new perspective. Today, however, my view was blocked as we rose through a thick layer of clouds.

Thankfully the pilot has a modern instrument panel that helps guide our course. Birds, too, have a sophisticated set of tools for navigation. Besides using landmarks during the day, they use the rotation of the stars, the orientation of Earth's magnetic field, and the angles of polarized light at sunset.

New research from the Max Planck Institute for Ornithology in Seewiesen, Germany, has added weight to the hypothesis that homing pigeons (and probably other birds) use smell to navigate home. Each place smells a little different, and breezes coming from different directions carry that information to the pigeons. The birds can essentially create a smell map in their head that helps them navigate back home. Amazing! But I'm still glad my pilot is using a GPS.

Although humans only achieved flight when they stopped trying to copy birds, now that we've figured it out, engineers are looking back at the more experienced flyers to solve all sorts of problems. For example, jet aircraft engines used to "choke" at supersonic speeds due to air moving around the engine instead of through it. The peregrine falcon—which can dive at more than 200 mph—provided a solution. Specialized cone-shaped bones near its nostrils, called baffles, deflect shockwaves of air and allow peregrines to keep breathing. Jets now have similar cones in their engines.

Despite the clouds, we found Chicago, and with our loon-like limited maneuverability, swung wide over the lake to start the landing pattern. As we slowed down and neared the ground, the plane used another bird-like feature on the wing. Slats on the front of the airplane's wings dropped down. According to Wikipedia, this "allows the wing to achieve a higher than normal angle of attack—and thus lift—without resulting in a stall."[4]

On a bird, the alula—a small projection on the leading edge of the wing—serves the same purpose. It is essentially the bird's thumb, and its three to five feathers can move freely. When flying slowly or landing, the bird can move the alula slightly upward and forward. It performs the same function as the airplane slats in slower or higher-angled flight.

Future airplanes may use a sharkskin-like paint job or butterfly scale-like coverings to reduce drag. Seabird-like moveable wings might improve resiliency to gusts. Humans continue to examine nature for more ways to improve flight. Even rubber made from Kazakh dandelions may one day provide a more sustainable material for landing gear.

As the old-fashioned rubber tires bumped onto the runway beneath me, I was grateful for the chance to view the world from a new perspective. I also realized that my relatively effortless trip was made possible by decades of innovation, just as the snow buntings' effortless grace rides on the wings of eons of evolution.

Flashes of Red

Susan Lewis

Now that the trees are stark and bare, things hidden from us all summer long become visible again. The angles of twigs are drawn precisely against the gray sky, with hornet nests, vireo nests, and oak galls as their only adornment. Withered ferns settle down to reveal the subtle shapes of the forest floor. Steel gray glimmers of open water weave their way through the trunks and remind me of places I have yet to explore.

The beauty of "stick season" as I learned to call it in

Vermont, is subtle to say the least. After leaves fall and before snow, the landscape is melancholy. It's easy to develop tunnel vision and stop noticing the woods. If we let them, these days of gray skies and brown ground can help us appreciate the bursts of color even more.

Have you seen the winterberry holly in the swamps? Bright red berries adorn every inch of every twig on female *Ilex verticillata* shrubs. The male flowers occur on separate plants and can't produce fruit themselves. Botanists and Greeks call this characteristic *dioecious*, meaning "two houses." Being low in fat, the berries last until late winter for two reasons: they don't go rancid quickly, and they aren't eaten until other more energy-dense fruits are scarce. Forty-nine species of birds eat those berries, from bluebirds and catbirds to our old friends the cedar waxwings.

I've seen other flashes of red lately, too—on my chilly cheeks, in holiday decorations, and on the crests of pileated woodpeckers. It's always thrilling to hear their wild laughing call and see the brilliant flash of their white wing linings as they swoop through forest clearings. My ornithology professor called them "monkeys of the Northwoods" because of their raucous call. Twice last week (when I was still braving twenty-degree dawns to bike to work), I saw a pair darting across Highway M and another pair on Garmisch Road.

Pileated woodpeckers mate for life and hold their territory year-round. The female who startled me yesterday morning by swooping in for lunch at the base of an oak tree outside my window was the same one I eagerly photographed from a second-story window last spring. You've probably noticed their large, rectangular holes in both softwood and hardwood trees. They'll drill anywhere they can find carpenter ants, which they extract with their sticky, foot-long tongue. Sometimes the hole is so large and the tree is so small that the trunk snaps right off!

It's no surprise that scientists and wildlife managers consider pileateds "ecosystem engineers." Especially beneficial is their aversion to using the same nest cavity twice. Every spring the pair will hollow out a new tree, often with two entrance holes, and the abandoned cavities are quickly repurposed by ducks, squirrels, owls, bats, other woodpeckers, and wasps. Pileated woodpeckers are the primary source of large tree cavities in the forest. It's as if one family in the neighborhood builds a new house every year and gives their old one away.

During the years of heavy logging near the turn of the last century, the populations of these crow-sized woodpeckers declined. As forests recovered, so did the birds. Though their numbers are slowly increasing, they still face hazards. In younger forests, pileateds tend to use the oldest, largest trees for their roosts. These taller trees are lightning rods and can be dangerous to the young families.

Once snow falls it will be easy to track the woodpeckers' eating habits. Fresh wood chips around the base of a tree—or in your ski tracks—are a good reminder to look up. Not only might you see a striking bird or their recent excavations, you will jolt yourself out of tunnel vision and be ready to notice the next burst of beauty in stick season.

Woolly Weather

Reese Leann Gbur, age 10

A blustery, fall wind swept away any warmth from the
pale sun. Brown and yellow leaves skittered across the
pavement. As I bent down to dip my hands in the lake,
my arm (wrapped in fuzzy fleece) brushed the seed head
of a burr marigold—so named because the cheery yellow
flower matures into a cluster of pokey, stick-tight seeds.

Distracted, I meandered back toward the car, picking little, two-pronged seeds out of my armpit as I went. Then . . . whoa! Something caught the corner of my eye, and I pulled my foot back from its next step. There in the middle of the parking lot, was a woolly bear caterpillar. Not the most exciting find, but it would have been unpleasant for us both if my shoe had continued on its original trajectory.

I've always enjoyed seeing these fuzzy, black- and brown-striped critters. As a kid I tortured them—poking one to watch it curl into a ball . . . patiently waiting until it uncurled . . . and then poking it again. You've probably had your own encounters with these cute little critters, no matter what age you happened to be.

Seeing this woolly bear didn't strike me as anything spectacular, but I took some photos anyway because a friend had asked me about the caterpillar's famed weather prediction skills. My research turned up a great story about that and so much more.

Back in 1948, Dr. C. H. Curran, curator of insects at the American Museum of Natural History in New York City, wanted an excuse to get out of the city and enjoy the fall colors. He decided that the question of woolly bears' weather prediction skills needed some field research (sounds like a great excuse to play hooky from work), and so he took his wife to a nearby state park. They gathered as many woolly bears as they could find and measured the sizes of the black and brown stripes. This was so fun that they invited friends the next year and began calling themselves The Original Society of the Friends of the Woolly Bear.

For eight years they "gathered data" in the beautiful fall woods. At first it seemed like they were onto something. Several years in a row, the brown stripes took up more than a third of the caterpillar's thirteen body segments, on average. Folklore says that wider brown stripes forecast milder winters, and that did indeed play out for Curran. Then came the year that two groups of caterpillars in neighboring habitats gave opposing forecasts. That year Curran gave up.

As it turns out, some scientists now think that the width of the brown band *is* related to the weather—of the previous spring. Each time the caterpillar gets too big for its skin and molts, one black segment changes to a brown segment. A woolly bear who starts eating early (they are generalist feeders who eat a variety of plants) during a mild spring will have a wider brown stripe by the following fall. A caterpillar who gets a late start, perhaps due to snow in April (not that we know anything about that!), will likely have fewer brown segments before the growing season ends again.

With one riddle solved, here's another. Why do you see so many woolly bears crossing the road this time of year? To get to an overwintering site! Like many northern critters (black bears and big brown bats, for example), woolly bears are short-distance migrants who need to travel a little way to find a nice place to spend the winter.

And they can get there fast (for a caterpillar) traveling at 0.05 miles an hour (about a mile a day).

Beneath a rock, under a log, in a bark crevice—almost any protected place will suffice for an overwintering woolly bear. Warmth is not a major factor since these little guys will freeze solid, thaw, and freeze again many times throughout the winter. On a warm day they may even get out and crawl around.

If a tomato spent the winter like a woolly bear, it would soon be mush. But woolly bears use chemicals known as cryoprotectants to safeguard living tissue against damage from freezing and thawing. Woolly bears who live in the Arctic (including the species we know as well as some relatives) may take 14 years to complete their life cycles. They freeze solid every winter and grow just a little bit during each brief summer.

This Northwoods woolly bear only needs two years to complete its life. In spring it will thaw and resume eating. Once large enough, the caterpillar spins itself a cocoon using silk and its own hairs. In two weeks it metamorphoses into a pale yellow Isabella tiger moth. In another two weeks the moth will mate, lay eggs, and die.

Tiger moths, in the family Arctiidae, are amazing, colorful creatures in their own right. Some tiger moth caterpillars eat toxic plants—just like monarch caterpillars—in order to protect themselves against predators. The toxin persists in the adult moths, who use bright warning coloration to tell potential predators that

they taste bad. Since one of their main predators—bats—
can't see colors in the dark, the moths also emit ultrasonic
sounds to warn bats of their unpalatability.

All the moths are surely dead by now, and their
offspring, the caterpillars, are racing toward their
overwintering rocks. I hope the one I almost stepped on
found a cozy place in the leaf litter. Although the woolly
bear can't give me an accurate forecast for the season to
come, it doesn't really matter—I overwinter in a house.

Late Fall Hike

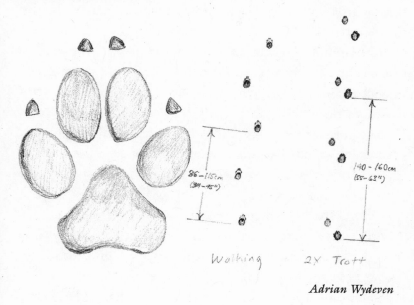

Walking   2X Trott

Adrian Wydeven

Despite the gray skies, despite the chilly wind, I needed
a hike. Already the wintery weather and lengthy darkness
had me down. Bike season was over for my sensitive toes;
ski season taunted me from just around the corner. I could
have curled up on the couch with a book, but I lured
myself out to the trail with memories of other times that a
walk in the woods had done me good.

An inch of snow covered the grassy, soggy ski trail.
Movement felt good, but my gray mood still clung. Soon
I began noticing tracks: the daisy chain of a grouse's small
steps, the dots and lines of a mouse dragging its tail, the

lacy pattern of a vole's diagonal walking gait, and the funny little half-tunnel of a shrew burrowing along the top of the grass.

The large, loping tracks of a fisher made me stop and look. Then barely ten steps down the trail, the belly-slide marks of an otter made me laugh as I imagined his playful mode of travel.

In summer the woods bustle with life, but the comings and goings of little feet are hard to decipher in the thick grass and leaves. The first snow primed the forest's typewriter and now the paw-and-claw-inked words were preserved for a moment, allowing me to read their stories.

Still the cabin fever was persistent. Mouse tracks became routine, and above trudging footsteps, my mind turned inward.

Then out of the corner of my eye . . . WOLVES! While my thoughts had been elsewhere, my eyes registered the big, four-toed paw prints scuffing the snow across a whole section of trail. I grinned, my mind now alert and senses primed. A quick survey of the scene allowed me to estimate: definitely four, probably five wolves.

Maybe you think I should have been nervous, walking in wolf-filled woods alone. I was not. Having tracked wolves in several different places (Minnesota, Yellowstone, and Wisconsin), and observed them for hours on end (they mostly slept), I was confident that their wildness and skittishness of humans kept me safe. I was fine with any risk that remained.

Instead of being nervous, I was thrilled. I love seeing evidence that such graceful, powerful predators inhabit these woods. I love knowing they were here—running easily, determinedly, and playfully through the forest. Perhaps if I had livestock, dogs, or children I would feel differently. Perhaps that's why I don't have them . . .

After seeing those tracks, I felt alert and alive. For the rest of the hike, I peered into the woods. Marcescent oak leaves fluttered. The clouds flushed pink in the setting sun. Nothing else happened. No wolves allowed me to see them.

Too soon I crossed my own large boot tracks near the trailhead. As I neared my car, I filed the hike away in my memory for another gray day when I need an extra incentive to lure me out for a walk in the woods.

Feathered Feast

Annaliese Collins, age 6

Thanksgiving Dinner was a raucous affair. Thousands of guests dove in head first, gobbling up the delicate greens and crustaceans. Some preferred crisp, white tubers or seeds and grains. Frog legs, fish, and escargot tempted the tastes of others. New arrivals joining the feast from the far north appreciated the mild weather and plentiful food. Some guests took breaks from eating to nap in a quiet, out–of–the–way area, while others bathed noisily nearby.

You may think my family is a bit odd, but we were not alone. A couple dozen other birdwatchers with spotting scopes and binoculars had also stationed themselves at various overlooks along the Mississippi River on

Thanksgiving Day. We chose the narrow, winding, graveled Red Oak Road just south of Lansing, Iowa, for our observation point. The road hugs a hillside above the railroad tracks, overlooking a marshy backwater of "Ol'Man River."

Nearly half of North America's bird species and about 40 percent of its waterfowl spend at least part of their lives in the Mississippi Flyway. It is a globally significant flyway that provides habitat for more than 325 species of birds. We spotted tundra swans, Canada geese, northern shovelers, northern pintails, hooded mergansers, canvasbacks, green-winged teal, ring-necked ducks, buffleheads, lesser scaup, wood ducks, mallards, and more. They dove, dabbled, floated, and napped in the early afternoon sun.

The Mississippi River's watershed covers 41 percent of the continental United States as it spreads across the heart of the nation. Still it is only one section of the longest migration route in the Western Hemisphere. The flyway continues north along the Mackenzie River in the Northwest Territories of Canada, finally reaching its northern terminus on the shore of the Arctic Ocean. While most birds only follow this route as far south as the Gulf of Mexico or Central America, some shorebirds fly all the way to Patagonia at the southern tip of South America.

Without warning, some mysterious danger startled the feasting birds, and about half of the dinner party took to the air, calling and honking wildly. The flash of sunlight on the tundra swans' white feathers was breathtaking. From their takeoff en masse, the flock divided into long strings and Vs, self-organizing according to avian guidelines I can't even imagine. Soon smaller groups of a dozen birds or fewer circled back and made their splash landings in the backwaters. The supposed danger must have passed or never materialized.

Unfortunately the coyote or eagle that may have startled the group might not be the biggest danger they face. Invasive species, pollution, flood control, droughts, land-use practices, and agricultural runoff all threaten the health of the river for both human and wildlife use. What will happen to this gorgeous, feathered spectacle in the future?

For today, none of those threats deterred the birds, and my family simply enjoyed the chance to stand in the sunshine and watch intercontinental travelers go about their amazing lives.

Inhale Beauty. Exhale Gratitude.

Thomas Karczewski, age 8

"The more you know about something, the more you see in it and the more beautiful it is." — Tom Fitz, Northland College geology professor

Sharp cold air flooded my lungs when I stepped outside this morning. A fresh dusting of snow glittered where the morning sun filtered through trees, and that same sun shone on rosy clouds in a blue sky. I took another breath. Inhale beauty. Exhale gratitude.

Crunch . . . crunch . . . crunch. With sunflower seeds cupped in my outstretched palm, I walked to a spot between the thicket of balsam fir trees and the empty bird feeder. The trees were silent—frozen by my movement. The hyperactive hopping of a single chickadee broke the stillness. Within seconds, the whole flock was back.

During the summer, black-capped chickadees focus on their mate and their chicks. Even if I didn't have to take my feeder down because of the bears, the birds wouldn't gather like this for a group feast. By late fall, chickadee flocks are well established and ready to defend a winter-feeding territory. One territory just happens to include my feeder.

Like wolf packs, chickadee flocks have alpha and beta pairs at the top of the hierarchy, other mated pairs below them, and then unmated juveniles at the bottom. Unlike wolves, the juveniles are not the offspring of pairs in the flock. Instead, their parents kicked them out of their childhood range in the hopes of spreading genetic diversity a little wider.

As I stood with my hand outstretched, I listened to the interactions of the flock. Dominant birds responded with aggressive gargles aimed at lower-ranked birds who got too close or disputed the ownership of a seed. Researchers have found that the gargler almost always wins the fight. Shy "tseet tseets" from hidden chickadees maintaining contact with the flock filtered through the thick boughs. Chick-a-dee-dee-dee calls could have been greetings to friends—or warnings about the possible danger of my presence.

The whirr of wing beats also filled the air as chickadees swooped bravely over my head to the empty feeder. From there they perched atop the broom handle near the door, clung to the side of the porch pillar with needle-like toes, and darted back to the safety of the fir boughs. None flew to my seed-filled hand, even though I hoped very intently.

Why wouldn't they jump at the chance to eat a few more seeds? In order to maintain their normal 108 degree body temperature, chickadees must eat the caloric equivalent of 250 sunflower seeds each day. They gain up to 10 percent of their body weight in fat each day and burn it off each night to stay warm.

Maybe the chickadees weren't hungry enough to brave my hand because they were raiding their cached food instead. Norwegian researchers found that the tit (a chickadee relative) caches up to 80,000 seeds in a single autumn. Unlike red squirrels who put all their seeds in one stump and then have to defend it fiercely, chickadees spread out their seeds singly and don't worry about a few getting stolen.

If I were a chickadee, my biggest source of seed loss would be my own forgetfulness! Chickadees have it figured out. They use forgetfulness to make space for new memories each year. Every fall, brain neurons containing old information die, and new neurons grow with current information about seed locations, social flocks, and their habitat.

This also means that they have forgotten my past role as a harmless provider of food. My hand throbbed with cold, so I stuck it back in my mitten and walked down to the lake for a break. Those rosy clouds and that blue sky sat reflected in a section of open water, surrounded by a skim of ice.

I continued down the driveway, stepping over the leaping tracks of red squirrels, the tiny bounds of mice, and the snowed-in trail of a midnight fox. All these brave creatures share the winter world with the chickadees and me.

Scooping seeds out from the tip of my mitten where I had stored them, I tried again. Standing silently, hand outstretched, I waited. Again the flock began swooping around me, but not landing. Then a different movement caught my eye—a vole was foraging at the base of the dead spruce.

The instant that my focus left the birds for the vole, I felt the spiny grip of a chickadee on my finger. Not daring to shift my gaze and scare it off, I kept my eyes on the vole and my awareness in that finger. I took a deep breath of crisp air. Inhale beauty. Exhale gratitude.

Now the spell was broken. Several more chickadees swooped down to grab seeds. Between visits I was able to look down. One chickadee cocked its head and peered up at me through a shiny black eye, as if to say, "I see you. You're okay." That was all I wanted.

WINTER

An Old Friend

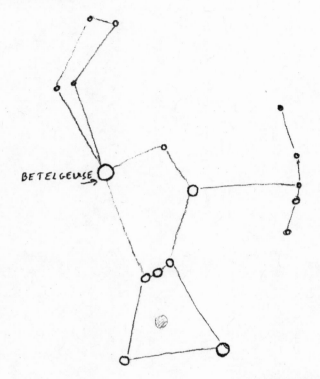

BETELGEUSE

Vivianne Hanke

The dark road curved beneath my headlights and then straightened into a long trough between the trees. An old friend lay resting there, just above the pointed tips of spruce and fir.

Orion has been my favorite winter constellation for many years. Sometimes subtitled "The Hunter," it seems apt that Orion is lying on his side tonight, resting up for an early morning of deer hunting. Traditionally, of course, his quarry was more mythical—chasing the beautiful Seven Sisters of Pleiades, doing battle with Taurus the Bull, fighting a scorpion sent to tame his ego, and hunting the constellation Lepus the Hare.

In Australia and New Zealand, Orion appears upside down, and his distinctive belt and sword are imagined to be a cooking pot instead. Perfect for the *end* of hunting season! Closer to home, some in the Ojibwa culture call this constellation Kabibona'kan, the Winter Maker, as its presence in the night sky heralds winter. Appropriately, he can be seen from November to February each year.

Of the four stars that form the rectangular shape of Orion's body, Betelgeuse is my favorite. This reddish-colored star forms Orion's right shoulder, assuming the hunter is facing us. The red color is not an optical illusion, and it is not due to rusty iron, as is the color of Mars. Betelgeuse is a type of star called a red supergiant, and it gives off most of its light in the near-infrared wavelength, which we cannot see. It is at the opposite end of the spectrum from ultraviolet light, which is also invisible to humans. Only a small portion (13 percent) of Betelgeuse's light is visible to our eyes.

Earlier this fall, I found out that if we could see ultraviolet light, we could tell male chickadees from females. This week I discovered that if we could see infrared light, Betelgeuse would be the brightest star in the sky. My narrow spectrum of human vision feels limiting, even disregarding that I have been nearsighted since third grade. What is amazing is that we have built surrogate eyes: instruments that can "see" these wavelengths and translate them into beautiful images in the visible spectrum of colors.

With the help of these instruments, astrophysicists have seen hotspots and other features on the surface of Betelgeuse. One astronomer characterized Betelgeuse as "an enormous seething restless caldron of belching plasma."

Something that violent can hardly last long. Indeed, Betelgeuse has already used up its supply of hydrogen for nuclear fusion. This means that heavier elements are fusing together, and the star's core is compressed into a hot, dense, ball, while other outer layers have expanded into the huge red mass we see today. Stars like this are rare— we only know of 200 in our galaxy—because they do not live very long.

At about 10 million years old, Betelgeuse is thought to be near the end of its life. It will likely explode into a supernova within the next million years. When it does, it will be visible even in the day—brighter than the moon— and to an outside observer would outshine the entire Milky Way Galaxy.

While I admire the superlative nature of stars like Betelgeuse, I often think about how wonderful our own star is. Our Sun is just the right size, just the right distance, just the right age, and just the right brightness to make life on Earth possible.

This time of year, when gray clouds can hang low for many days in a row, a splash of sunlight on my face feels like gift. I am even grateful for when the sun is not around. Crystalline stars and shimmering Northern Lights appear closer in these long winter nights. This time of year, Orion is really a perfect friend. He keeps me company on dark, lonely drives, sparkles handsomely above my doorstep, and after hobnobbing with him, I can still get to bed early.

On the Edge

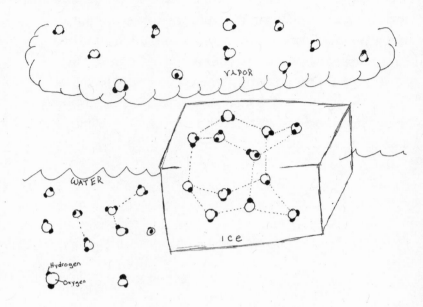

Heather Edvenson

This morning I drove toward the edge of the earth. Moment after moment I approached the end of the pavement, only to see the world emerge from thick, white nothingness and reveal itself before me.

A bit dramatic, perhaps, for describing a foggy morning in early winter, but such was the mood of the light. The morning was part beauty, part eerie, and part mystery. Frosty fields and forests zoomed by on either side, and a pallid sun—somewhere above the world's ceiling—found the strength to make them sparkle.

I've had the feeling lately that we are living on the edge of the seasons. Any moment now the puddles will freeze and stay frozen. The frosty grass will not darken and melt under the low-slung sun and will instead disappear under thickening layers of snowflakes.

Water itself is living on the edge these days, the edge of phase transitions from gas, to liquid, to solid. Each of these transitions results from changes in temperature and energy levels. Heat is the energy of molecules in motion, and thus the phase of water is directly related to its temperature, an indicator of heat energy.

Our daily temperatures fluctuate from just below to just above the freezing point of water. Each night when Orion presides over icy stars, the temperature on Earth drops. At the dew point, water molecules in the gaseous state slow down enough to condense into liquid water droplets suspended in the air. Clouds of fog appear near the damp earth. The invisible gas becomes visible, but it conceals the solid world. Gas to liquid.

The same thing happened as my teapot whistled cheerily, expelling hot water vapor that condensed into visible steam in the chilly kitchen. Taking my mug of tea, I went down to the lake where a fragile layer of ice hugged the shore. It was so thin that I could barely see the ice itself. Only the unnatural stillness on the surface, or a tap with my toe, betrayed the ice's presence. The lake is on the edge of something, too.

Most of the lake is now at about 39 degrees Fahrenheit,

the temperature at which water reaches its maximum density. Under Orion's watchful gaze, the surface water's temperature will drop farther—and begin to float. This colder water will accumulate until it reaches the magical 32 degrees Fahrenheit. Then molecules align, crystals form, and the lake receives its winter lid. Liquid to solid.

When the dew point is below the freezing point, water vapor transitions directly from gas to solid in the form of frost on solid surfaces. High in the sky, where the only solid surfaces are grains of dust, the frost becomes flakes. Ice crystals form directly from water vapor in the air using dust as condensation nuclei. A snowflake's complex sixfold symmetry is guided by the chemical properties of water. As incipient snowflakes travel around within a cloud, more ice crystals condense on their facets, and their growth is influenced by the temperature and humidity of the air. The best snowflakes grow at 5 degrees Fahrenheit inside dense, humid, winter clouds. Gas to solid.

No snowflakes fell today. Blue sky shone through as the fog bank lifted. Energy from the Sun heated the air and it expanded, increasing the amount of water it could hold. Water droplets suspended in the fog evaporated and become invisible again, revealing that my path leads not toward nothingness, but into a fantastically decorated fairytale world. Even more amazing is that, as I tell my students, "It's like magic, but actually it's chemistry."

Life under the Ice

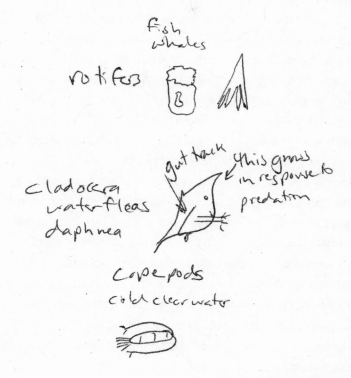

fish
whales

rotifers

gut track   this grows
             in response to
             predation

cladocera
waterfleas
daphnea

copepods
cold clear water

Field trip notes, Emily Stone

Nets in hand, a line of Wisconsin Master Naturalist students ventured onto the dock. Snowflakes danced on the wind as a prelude to the big snowstorm yet to come. For now the thin ice in the marina by Barker's Island in Superior, Wisconsin, held a layer of snow just one flake thick. Dr. Joel Hoffman of the Environmental Protection Agency had broken open a narrow channel in the ice parallel to the dock and was ready to help us discover a hidden world.

Underneath the snow-free ice, he explained, enough sunlight penetrates that life continues as usual. But what is usual for a harbor connected to Lake Superior? Our nets were made of 150 micron mesh. One micron (or micrometer or µm) is a millionth of a meter. We sure weren't trying to catch fish! A Northland College student sampled with one diamond-shaped net. This plankton net was designed to be lowered to the bottom of the lake and drawn straight up. It provides a cross section of the entire water column. John Kudlas, a steadfast Museum volunteer and educator, used another net affixed to a long handle to sample one layer of water with a horizontal sweep.

The particles in the bottom of the nets didn't look particularly lively to our naked eyes. Most of the organisms that Joel expected us to find are only about 1–2 mm long. We brought them in out of the chill, rinsed the samples onto Petri dishes, and put them under dissecting microscopes.

The makeshift office of the brand-new Lake Superior National Estuarine Research Reserve erupted with enthusiasm. "Wow! Cool! Oh my gosh, look at this! Joel, what's this? Did you see that? Check out what I've got. Here's a good one! Oh it just moved. You've gotta see this!"

Copepods, cladocerans, and rotifers, oh my! Tiny aliens swam, spun, and ate before our eyes. Joel had drawn diagrams on the board of what we might see, and now they came alive.

Copepods were some of the most common critters in our samples. These tiny crustaceans live in the sea and in nearly every freshwater habitat (including the lake right outside your door). Their teardrop-shaped bodies are covered by an exoskeleton so thin that it is transparent, and they are adorned with large antennae and a single red eye. Bristle-like setae do most of their sensing and can differentiate patterns in the water flow around their body caused by approaching predators or prey. Some copepods have extremely fast escape responses when they sense a predator, and they can spring a few millimeters out of the way.

Such small creatures do not need a circulatory system. One group, the calanoid copepods, have a heart but no blood vessels. Most lack gills and let oxygen absorb directly into their bodies. The copepod larval form is even simpler, consisting only of a head and a small tail, with no thorax or abdomen. A larvae must molt five to six times before it attains a complete set of body parts. After five more molts, it reaches adulthood. This process can take anywhere from a week to a year, depending on the species, temperature, and food availability.

Some scientists say that copepods form the largest animal biomass on Earth. Since copepods use carbon to create their exoskeletons (discarding ten or more exoskeletons over their lives) and release carbon into the ocean through respiration and scat, they are important to the global carbon cycle. The upper layers of the ocean are the world's largest carbon sink and can absorb one third of humans' annual carbon emissions.

Several copepods ate their carbon-based lunch as awed students spied through the scopes. Their mouthparts swished the water to create currents that drew food toward their bristly setae. Large particles were individually caught by "fling and clap" movements, where appendages grasped both the particle and a packet of water surrounding it and removed the water by an inward squeeze.

All too soon, the students returned the samples to the lake. The snow fell harder. With less sunlight filtering through the ice and snow, life in the lakes will slow down a bit for the winter. Some critters enter resting stages; others just slow their metabolisms. As you look out over the frozen lakes, can you imagine tiny, translucent copepods living in their hidden world?

Crossbills and Irruptions

Jenni Thomson

Winter often brings interesting things down from the
north. Snow, for one, floats in on cold arctic air that
sweeps in from Canada. Earlier in the fall, we saw many
migrating birds on their way south for the winter.
They stop in our wetlands and forests to eat and rest.
We may also notice retired "snowbirds" migrating
on the same routes, zooming along in vehicles and
refueling at the nearest service station. Many birds—and

snowbirds—migrate along the same routes every year, and their timing is so precise that phenologists (people who study the timing of seasonal natural events) can predict the arrival of the first and the departure of the last of each species to within a few days.

Other species are not so orderly and seem to migrate helter-skelter in regards to date and location. Snowy owls, redpolls, and crossbills are a few examples of these "irruptive species." To irrupt means to *enter* an area suddenly, in contrast to the lava erupting *out* of the volcano. We don't see these irruptive species every winter, at least not in any quantity. Food availability drives most migrations, and these are no different. Have you ever noticed that our fair-weather bird friends are the ones who eat a lot of insects, especially flying insects? Think of all those warblers, flycatchers, and vireos—they skedaddle about the time I put away my insect repellant.

Our year-round residents tend to eat seeds or meat, which are easier to find in the winter than mosquitoes. Goldfinches and house finches are seedeaters whom we can enjoy all winter long. Chickadees must eat the energy equivalent of about 250 sunflower seeds per day in winter! They don't just eat seeds, though. You may have seen them at your suet feeder or pecking at the fat on roadkill deer.

Crossbills are finches that can survive almost anywhere and nest in any season as long as they have plenty of spruce or tamarack seeds. They are a classic irruptive species.

Crossbills are fascinating creatures. Just as their name suggests, their bills are crossed. The lower mandible curves under the upper mandible. They can be either "right-beaked" or "left-beaked," but just as in humans, right-beaked birds are more common.

To eat, the crossbill slips its slightly open beak under the tightly shingled scales of spruce cones and then closes its bill using strong biting muscles. The scale lifts up just enough for the crossbill to grab the seed with its tongue. Crossbills often twist a cone off the tree and take it to a perch. They extract seeds from the bottom of the cone up, while holding the cone in one foot and rotating it like an ear of corn. A single crossbill can eat up to 3,000 seeds a day!

During this time of year, it is common for flocks of humans to irrupt as well, often congregating in large and gregarious flocks where there is plenty of food. As winter closes in, we are reminded about what it means to share the bounty of this beautiful Earth and to give thanks for all we have.

Marks

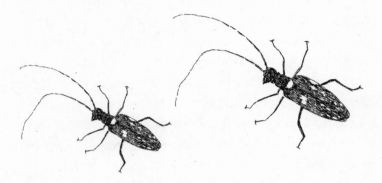

Caroline Perkins

Even as I parked my car at the trailhead, my eyes were alert for tracks in the slushy snow. Although the parking lot itself was almost snow free, little plops of mush marked where a dog and their person had walked through the snow, compacting it underneath and pushing snow out to the sides of their soles. The denser snow of their tracks melted more slowly and left a curious pattern of raised tracks on the damp pavement. Such small actions can make the difference between solid or liquid water at this time of year.

After examining the tracks, I walked up the leaf-strewn and snow-lined path toward the North Country Trail. I had never been to this section—just north of Lake Owen—and it was beautiful! Soon I noticed curious tracks in the deeper snow on the side of the trail. A five-pointed crown of toes topped an oblong footpad. The impressions of the hind feet were almost as big as my hand. In one spot I could see a faint trough from the otter's belly slide.

Farther along, a skinnier trough, only an inch or so wide, crossed the trail between a fallen log and the base of a big white pine. Tiny voles and shrews make these channels in the snow, often burrowing beneath the drifts when they are deep enough. This time, their furry little backs may have been exposed to the watchful eyes of a raptor. But luckily for the small mammal, there were no signs of attack.

At the base of another tree—a dead maple—lay the scattered chips from a frenzied woodworker. Smaller holes, just over an inch in diameter, accented a long, vertical groove where the pileated woodpecker chiseled into the center of the tree. While we may want to blame the bird for the damage, it was only feeding on the carpenter ants who had already colonized the tree. Since the ants eat interior wood that has already been retired from transporting water and nutrients, a tree can survive for a long time while being hollowed out by ants and their predators.

Around another corner I found a tree with a completely different injury: a huge white pine was twisted and splintered across the path. Here was another tracking medium. Many insects had inscribed their stories in the woody scroll.

Most striking at first were the eight-millimeter diameter exit holes of adult sawyer beetles. On a warm July day, an odd-looking creature had emerged from the perfectly round hole. Aptly nicknamed the longhorn beetle, a male's antennae can be twice the length of his body. Those antennae contain chemical receptors that are finely tuned to finding stressed or recently dead trees. Although it may just smell like pine to us, the beetle smells dinner and the potential for romance.

After adult sawyer beetles mate and lay eggs on a dead tree (live trees would defend themselves by covering the insects in sticky, turpentine resins), the larvae burrow into the tree to feed on the phloem and cambium layers. This inner bark of the tree is responsible for sugar transport and growth, and contains more nutrients than the dead, hollow tubes of the xylem (sapwood) that carry mostly water. Shallow, wiggling furrows, ending in small, dark holes, marked the beetles' feeding progress on this fractured white pine.

In early fall the sawyer beetle larvae begin to excavate clear through to the center of the trunk with a scraping, sawing sound. Just like the woodpecker, they leave behind a trail of splintery frass that is not ingested. Next summer, they will exit through much larger holes, like the ones I noticed first.

Nearby on a dead balsam fir, smaller bark beetles had inscribed their life stories as well. Deeper horizontal burrows carved by the adults were punctuated by tiny round chambers like a string of pearls. The female would have laid an egg where there now was a round chamber. After hatching, the larvae burrowed up a bit, toward the

surface, and excavated shallower channels at right angles
to their mother. When mature, they all backtracked out
the entrance hole made by the father.

The light faded as I turned back toward the trailhead.
Hurrying along to beat the sunset, I noticed that the
trail itself was in a depression that closely resembled
the belly track of the otter, the trough of the shrew, the
woodpecker's lunch counter, and the beetle's burrows.
How many feet have carved this trough, and what are
their life stories?

In many small ways we each leave our mark on the world.

Tracking Stories

Brynn Johnson, age 11

This morning I followed my fox down the hill to the lake. By "followed" I mean I walked next to his footprints, and by "my" fox I only mean the local one who lays dainty, beaded necklaces of tracks all over my yard and across my doorstep. In the delicate trails that he weaves through hemlocks, along fallen logs, to and from the compost pile, and zigzagging down the driveway, I read a life filled with purpose and joy.

The recent snows make a perfect tracking medium, and noticing tracks can make the woods come alive. Last week, behind the garage, I found a mess of the fox's tracks around a small lump of leaves covered in snow. Two bright yellow dabs of urine indicated that this was a scent mound, used for marking his territory. Male members of the dog family, Canidae, will use raised leg urination to let others in the area know that this territory is taken and defended.

It sounds crazy, but I got down on my hands and knees and sniffed the urine. Red fox and gray fox urine each have their own unique scents. Both are slightly skunky, but the red fox smells much sharper and stronger while the gray fox's scent is mellower. The smell test confirmed that I've been tracking a gray fox. This scent marking is also why I've been referring to my neighbor as "he." By the end of last winter, I had noticed enough side-by-side fox trails to be confident that my yard housed a pair of foxes. I don't have enough evidence yet to be sure that the female is still around, but this is the beginning of mating season, so I may know soon.

Back at the lake, I found a gray fox highway. Perforating the snow were at least eight different sets of tracks going in many directions along the edge of the ice and up onto shore. One of the trails was very different—definitely not a fox.

Large (as long as my entire pointer finger) and with five toes arranged asymmetrically, these tracks bounded along the bank in the 2x pattern. This is a common track pattern in the Mustelidae or weasel family. I can find half-inch tracks from the least weasel all the way up to four-inch tracks from the river otter and fisher bounding two-by-two down trails in this area. Each set of tracks is the result of the back feet landing precisely in the prints left by the front feet.

Being so close to the lake, I expected the animal to break into a slide at any moment. River otters will often belly slide over leaves, mud, ice, or snow, leaving long, foot-wide troughs between tight groups of tracks. I quickened my pace as I followed the trail over logs, down near alders on the shore, and under balsam fir branches. Not once did they break from the 2x pattern. In my notebook I would record these large weasel tracks as "likely fisher." These large, dark brown weasels, with a reputation for being inquisitive and ferocious, are an important predator of porcupines in the region. Hunters often share stories of seeing fishers while sitting quietly.

Tracking is always a "probably" kind of game. Any animal can do any gait, and foot size overlaps among many species. While habitat, behavior, scat, kill sites, and many other clues can help with identification, there is always an element of uncertainty. The sense of a mystery that might not be solved is what keeps me hooked.

Black and White

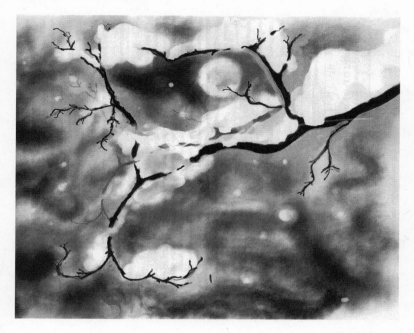

Nanette Rasmussen

Frosty air stung my cheeks, and my breath froze on my eyelashes as I zoomed down the trail. Fading sunlight and frigid temperatures haven't kept me from skiing. An intricate pattern of blacks and whites decorated the thick winter woods. Each twig carried a shadow of white snow. Wind-driven crystals accentuated the furrowed bark of trees. Subtle shadows graced the drifted terrain. I was skiing through an Ansel Adams photograph.

Pale sunlight gradually faded behind the hills, and a gibbous moon rose to take its place. I barely noticed the change in light at first, since the Moon (reflecting rays from the Sun back toward us) was so bright. During the long days of summer—when bedtime comes before twilight, and mosquitoes flock at dusk—I seldom get outside after dark. Skiing under the stars, with trees casting moon shadows across my path, was a lovely treat. The contrast between trees and snow made it easy to navigate. I left my headlamp in my pocket.

As my purple mittens swung in an easy rhythm, I noticed their color fading toward charcoal gray, finally matching the color scheme of the forest. Despite being mostly limited to seeing in gray scale now, it was still impressive that I could see at all. According to the American Optometric Association, the sensing capabilities of the human eye reach across nine orders of magnitude. This means that the dimmest light we can see is one-billionth as bright as the brightest light we can see.

Two different types of light receptors in our eyes make this possible. Our cone cells function in daylight and give us color vision with a high resolution of detail (20/20 vision if you're lucky). Rod cells work even in very dim light but provide limited resolution (20/200 vision) and a black and white palette. Cones are clustered in the center of our retinas while rods form a donut around the periphery of the retina.

A freaky side effect of the rod and cone arrangement is that if I stare directly at a small object in the dark, it will disappear! A tree trunk might be severed with its top half floating, my friend's face might go dark, or a star I just saw might blink out. These optical illusions are caused by a small blind spot in the middle of my night vision, where the cones would focus if they had sufficient light. If I just look slightly to the side, the objects will reappear.

Humans have several additional adaptions that help us to see across such a wide spectrum of light levels. Our pupils can dilate to let in more light at night or contract to physically protect our eyes from damaging amounts of light during the day. The diameter of the pupil can shrink to 1.5 millimeters and expand to 8 millimeters, which equates to a thirty-fold range in the quantity of light entering the eye. After skiing for more than half an hour in low light conditions, my pupils were widely dilated.

A chemical called rhodopsin is another key to night vision. Rods use rhodopsin to absorb photons and perceive light by converting it to electrical activity, which initiates visual impulses in the brain. (Cones use their own specific photopigment in the same way.)

When eyes are exposed to bright light, photons split the rhodopsin into two other chemicals. This reduces the sensitivity of our retina and protects our eyes from damage due to intense light. It also diminishes our ability to see in low light. For example, turning on a flashlight temporarily ruins our night vision. Although it takes several minutes, the chemicals eventually recombine into rhodopsin and our night vision returns.

The moonlight provided plenty of light for skiing. Rods

can function even on an overcast night with no moon, and the high contrast between snow and trees gave me confidence in avoiding collisions. As moon shadows from the trees slipped by, I looked down to admire the patterns. I was surprised to find that my skis still looked red!

Back inside, I did a little research and discovered that with any color except red, as we turn down the lights, we can watch while the color first turns gray (when the cones stop working), and then we lose the sensation of light (when rods stop working). This is called the photochromatic interval. With red, however, the color and sensation of light disappear at the same time. And, as it turns out, cones can function a little even with only 50 percent moonlight!

With winter solstice and the shortest days of the year behind us, every day yields increasing amounts of light to illuminate our adventures. For now, our grayscale night vision melds perfectly with the black-and-white winter world. By summer—when our cones have more light to see by—the Northwoods will once again be full of color.

Shrewd

Victoria Zalatoris

A brisk wind bit my cheeks as we hiked down the trail. Even bundled up in a puffy jacket and thick pants, with a wool hat on my head and jumbo mittens on my hands, I could not keep my nose and toes from getting cold. Three to four inches of snow crunched loudly under our boots. Most of the dimples in the snow were made by raindrops or tree-falling snow plops, but a few were made by wild little feet.

The daisy chain tracks of a grouse crisscrossed the trail like a holiday garland. Imprints from hopping squirrels connected trees like strings of lights. One trail decoration was slightly different. Marked by a subtle change in the color of the snow, it was simply a one-inch thick line across the path.

Curious, I knelt down and poked through the snow with my fingers. They found a hollow beneath the icy crust. Sliding my fingers under the crust, following the two-finger-wide line of gray, I peeled the crystalline roof off a long, narrow tunnel. In the frozen slush on the tunnel's floor were tiny footprints in a diagonal walking pattern.

Was this the secret passageway of a forest sprite or snow fairy? The hallway of snow would certainly protect its travelers from the bitter wind that reddened my cheeks.

No, not a fairy, but this tunnel belonged to a forest sprite in its own right—a shrew. There are six species of shrews in Wisconsin, and they are all tiny. Short legs, a pointed nose, slender body, and small eyes and ears help shrews function at the interface between soil particles and plant debris. They use their acute sense of smell—and even echolocation—to find food. This habitat is rich with their favorite prey: insect larvae, ants, beetles, crickets, grasshoppers, spiders, centipedes, slugs, and snails.

Shrews have an extraordinarily fast metabolism and digest their food very rapidly, so they must feed voraciously night and day. A shrew can only last a few hours without food and must eat more than its body weight in a 24-hour period. One species of shrew, the short-tailed shrew, has developed venomous saliva that can stun larger animals such as mice, rabbits, and cats. This allows them access to larger meals.

The venom may also help protect the short-tailed shrew from its many predators: bigger shrews, owls, hawks, snakes, frogs, and fish. Large mammals like foxes, weasels, and bobcats may kill and eat shrews, but often leave them on the ground, presumably because of the species' strong odor. Deb Nelson, the director of the Cable Natural History Museum, shared a story about her indoor/outdoor cat, OhOh, projectile vomiting a shrew across the living room as Deb dived to catch it in a wad of paper towels. What does that say about the palatability of shrews?

Palatable or not, most shrews die within the first year, if not the first two months of life. We found one of those casualties outside the Museum's back door just the other day. Whether death came by starvation or a predator, the result was the same. I carefully measured the body, tail, and hind feet to help me identify it as a masked shrew, *Sorex cinereus,* the most widely distributed shrew in North America. It is in a different genus than the short-tailed shrew, and is not reported to have a venomous bite.

As I examined the rigid, furry corpse I was astonished by its diminutive size and weight. Measuring less than four inches from nose to tail and weighing less than a penny, it is amazing that this critter can survive a Wisconsin winter.

At that size, staying warm can be tough. The subnivean layer, where snow meets earth, remains at a relatively constant 32 degrees. While this may not seem tropical to you, compared to a negative 10 degree windchill topside, it is a significant improvement. Deeper snow means more insulation from the skyward elements, so I bet shrews love snowier winters, just like skiers.

Along the trail, the tracks grew indistinct, and the wind picked up as the gray skies grew darker. On this cold winter afternoon, I would not have minded a calm, cozy tunnel for myself.

Ode to the Glaciers

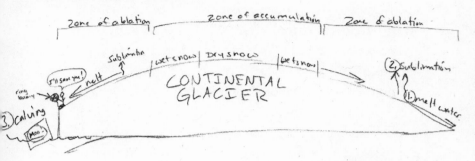

Lecture notes, Emily Stone

What do you love most about the Northwoods? Rolling hills traversed by some of the best trails in the country, winding back roads, sparkling lakes, and shady green forests are some of my favorite features. Have you ever wondered why all these wonderful things come together in northern Wisconsin? Maybe you know that this region was shaped by glaciers, but have you ever really sat down and appreciated all that the glaciers did for us?

I love glaciers. I've only ever seen one in person (Grinnell Glacier in Glacier National Park), and yet they have vastly improved my quality of life. Whether you realize it or not, you also experience the joys of glaciers whenever you whiz down a rolling ski trail, hike merrily up and down hills, enjoy the stomach-dropping exhilaration of catching air on your snowmobile, or boat and fish on one of our many lakes.

The landscape around Cable and Hayward was shaped during the Wisconsin glaciation (named for us!) of the

Quaternary ice age (which is still going on in Greenland and Antarctica). It began about 100,000 years ago and hit its maximum extent about 21,000 years ago; the last glacier retreated out of Wisconsin into Canada by 10,000 years ago.

The very recent (geologically speaking) visit of a glacier here has had a profound impact on the local landscape. As glaciers advanced across the surface, they scraped, carved, and plucked rocks from their path and carried them along within the ice mass. Like a conveyor belt, the glaciers brought tons of sediment south with them. Two lobes of ice flowed into our area, and their lateral margins met somewhere near Lake Namakagon.

When it really started to get interesting is when the climate warmed and the ice began to melt faster here at its toe than new snow from Canada could replenish it. Huge chunks of ice were left behind from the melting edges of the glacier, and glacial outwash rivers carrying meltwater and debris off the glacier buried those ice cubes. Well insulated, the ice lay hidden under a flat surface of sand, gravel, and cobbles for many years.

Once the buried ice chunks melted, basins of all shapes and sizes were left behind where the ice had been. Sometimes these basins—called kettles—filled with water and became lakes. Some lakes then filled with peat and became bogs. Others are perched far above the water table and stay bone dry. This landscape of sandy, rocky soil pockmarked by kettles is called a "pitted outwash

plain." The Rock Lake ski and mountain bike trails east
of Cable are a prime example of this topography, and in
my opinion, a prime place for recreation because of it.
The American Birkebeiner Ski Trail takes advantage of the
varied terrain so effectively that its hills are legendary.

In places the glacial conveyor belt stagnated for a while,
leaving a line of jumbled sediment where its margin had
been. This is probably what created the wacky shoreline
of Lake Namakagon with many shallow bays and plentiful
fish habitat.

Even the towering spectacle of Mount Telemark owes
its existence to the glaciers. Rivers flowing on top of the
melting ice poured rocks into a large crevasse. When the
glacier melted, it left behind a 1,700-foot-tall pile of sand
called a "kame." It is the tallest kame in Wisconsin.

Not only did the glaciers shape our physical landscape,
they, by extension, continue to impact the human uses of
it. Unlike regions to the south and north, the Cable area
doesn't have extensive farming. Not only are there too
many hills, but the soil just keeps growing more rocks.
First, water percolates underneath buried rocks. When it
freezes, the ice crystals lift up the bigger rocks and sand falls
underneath. Over many freeze-thaw cycles, the rocks come
to the surface. Happily, many trees grow just fine in this
type of soil, so our local crops are forests instead of corn.

The next time you're out for a spin on a lake, road, or
trail in the Northwoods, take a moment to appreciate the
legacy of the glaciers.

Seeing Things

Donna Post

As I came around the corner, a dark blob at the edge of the road caught my eye. You know how we are always seeing things that aren't there? Mailbox reflectors morph into deer's eyes in our headlights. Tall stumps look like black bears. Clumps of leaves take on the shape of an owl. This dark blob was less than three feet tall. Its pointy ears and a sloped back were silhouetted against the bright, white snow. Then, in an instant, it leaped back into the tangled thicket of firs.

Bobcats aren't rare in Wisconsin, but I've only found one set of their tracks in all the miles of trails I've hiked and skied here. Seeing an animal make tracks is an excellent learning opportunity, so I stopped the car in an open stretch of road, put on the blinkers, and went over to check out the disturbed snow. Since the flakes were light and fluffy, none of the four toes were visible in the tracks. I could tell where the wild feline had walked calmly up to the edge of the road, sat down for a bit, and then hurried off with big, poufy bounds.

If I hadn't seen the actual cat, I don't think I could have identified its tracks. I *could* tell—by the size of the body and size of the tracks—that this was not a lynx. Canada lynx, with their four-inch wide, snowshoe-like feet, have never been abundant in Wisconsin since they prefer the deep snow and thick conifer habitat of their favorite prey—snowshoe hares. In some years, when the snowshoe hare population in Canada crashes, lynx will wander down to Wisconsin to find food. There hasn't been a sighting in Wisconsin since 1992, and there are only twenty-eight verified records since 1870. Because lynx are so rare here, they are listed as a protected wild animal, but not as a state endangered species. They are on the federal list of threatened and endangered wildlife. Bobcats can be trapped and hunted.

A few weeks ago in Minnesota's Cascade River State

Park, I watched as a bobcat walked up the trail toward me. It chose a soft place in the pine needles and lay down for a catnap, or perhaps it was waiting in ambush for a squirrel. Some minutes later it stood and stretched. Maybe it wasn't hunting as much as digesting, since it paused then to squat and deposit a long, dark, hair-filled scat. With that business taken care of, it walked daintily down the trail. A string of oval tracks just smaller than my lip balm were pressed into the light dusting of snow.

Do you believe me? I watched it happen, just like a movie, in my mind's eye. The body print was *just so* on the pine needles; the four tracks of a squatting position had an extra sharpness due to pressure and time. The scat was positioned exactly where you'd expect it to be.

Was I seeing things? Absolutely. That is the very essence of tracking.

Subnivean Chronicles

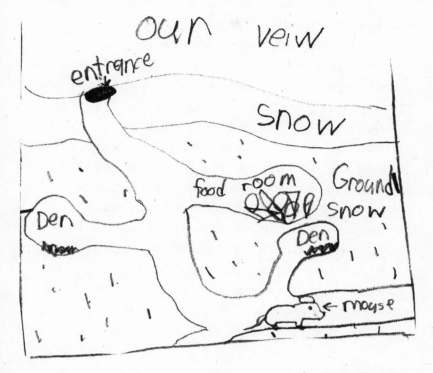

Mason McKay, age 10

Lately adventures in the woods have revealed fewer species than earlier in the winter. Tracking stories these days are mostly written by little feet, and many of the stories lay hidden below the surface. Now that there is a thickness of snow on the ground, a new world has formed. This ephemeral habitat is called the subnivean layer. Since I first learned about this hidden zone as a bright-eyed college freshman, it has taken on a mythical quality in my imagination. *Subnivean* sounds like it could be a region of Narnia ruled by the White Witch or perhaps an outpost neighboring Rivendell in Middle-earth.

The subnivean layer, like so much of life on Earth, owes its existence to the unique chemistry of water. When frozen, water becomes light and airy; it is a wonderful insulator. Just as down feathers in a jacket trap a layer of air next to the body—retaining the heat—a six-inch layer of snow traps air that retains heat from the earth. We don't have hot-rock geothermal here. There are no geysers or hot springs. Our ground warmth comes not from radioactive decay in the Earth's core, but simply from sunlight absorbed into the upper layers of soil and stone.

Because of this insulation and radiating warmth, a thin zone opens up under the snow, right at the surface of the ground. As water freezes, it releases a bit of heat, and as it melts, it absorbs a bit of heat. In this way the temperature in the subnivean zone is regulated at a relatively stable 32 degrees Fahrenheit. Compared to negative 20 degrees with a 15-mile-per-hour wind at the surface, that feels balmy!

Many tracks are now being pressed invisibly into the leaf litter that carpets the subnivean layer. Shrews, voles, and mice depend on this habitat for food, warmth, and protection from predators. Their presence is betrayed when the tiny jumping tracks of a deer mouse connect small trees with fallen logs. The half-inch-wide tunnel of a shrew will pop out at the edge of a ski trail or where snowshoes have packed down a trough. Sometimes shrews and voles will even tunnel through the surface of the snow—especially the fluffy stuff—leaving a winding channel that eventually descends through a portal into the snug subnivean layer.

Although soft, concealing snow may seem like a perfect security blanket, the fat, juicy prey are not safe from their wily and well-adapted predators. Owls can hear mice through the snowpack, triangulate the sound with their asymmetrical ears, and bust through the crust with fisted talons. Foxes and coyotes can also hear and pounce through the crust, thus securing a meal without even seeing it. Our three smallest weasel species—long-tailed, short-tailed, and least—are long and skinny with short legs for a reason. They can snake their way through mouse and chipmunk tunnels to catch the critters right in their own dens. Then the weasel will feast and nap at the warm hearth of its meal before resuming to search every tree, log, rock, and stump for another tasty treat.

Squirrel tracks connecting trees to small holes littered with leaf shards and pinecone scales are also prolific. Red squirrels will tunnel through the snow to find food caches stored last fall, and they often put a big hole in the ski track in the process.

Grouse also make use of the warm blanket that snow provides. When the snow is deep enough, they may "roost" by doing a swan dive into a drift, leaving no tracks that would lead a predator to their warm bed. In bad weather a grouse may stay in its burrow for a few days. Backcountry skiers and snowshoers tell stories of grouse flushing from these secret burrows just inches in front of their next step.

While many tracking stories lie hidden these days, it's fun to imagine the complex chronicles unfolding in the subnivean world. What lies beneath the smooth, white surface? More than we will ever know.

Predator and Prey

Victoria Zalatoris

Ice pellets stung my cheeks as I whizzzzzed down a steep slope. This roller coaster hill at the Rock Lake ski trails zoomed me all the way up to the top of the next knoll. As I glided over the crest and begin to pick up speed on the next downhill, I noticed tracks in the fluffy snow on the side of the trail.

On several previous occasions, I have purposely wiped out so I could go back and look at tracks, but just a quick look at these allowed me to guess their maker. The tracks showed two feet, each less than an inch wide, planted side by side, one slightly ahead of the other and with an impressively long leap between pairs of tracks. Must be a weasel.

We have three small weasels in Wisconsin—the least weasel (the world's smallest carnivore!), the short-tailed weasel, and the long-tailed weasel. Males are quite a bit bigger than females in each species, so a male short-tailed weasel could be just as big as a female long-tailed weasel. I could not identify these tracks to species, but all three share some amazing characteristics.

As extremely active critters with heart rates of up to 500 beats per minute and correspondingly high metabolisms, weasels must eat about 30 percent of their bodyweight each day. Fortunately they are adaptable predators. Rabbits, mice, and other small rodents are favorite prey, and weasels will even follow mice into their burrows. A flexible spine allows weasels to maneuver easily in tight spaces; sensitive whiskers and an excellent sense of smell guide weasels in the underground darkness; and taking over the den of their prey saves them the effort of digging their own burrow. While this may seem a bit harsh, weasels are important predators who help keep rodent populations in check.

Weasels are not at the top of their food chain and risk becoming prey to hawks, owls, snakes, house cats, foxes and more. Luckily protective coloration gives them an advantage in the snow. Weasels completely shed their fur and grow a new coat twice a year. As autumn days grow short, one transition begins. If temperatures are cold enough, a white coat grows in. If the temperature is warmer, or variable, the coat may have patches of white and brown. This helps the weasels adapt to variable weather patterns and new habitats. The lengthening days of spring trigger the transition to their brown summer coat.

Through all seasons, short-tailed and long-tailed weasels wear black tips on their tails. Instead of sticking out like a sore thumb, compromising their camouflage, the black tips actually provide an excellent distraction for their predators. In 1982 Roger A. Powell did an ingenious study at the Brookfield Zoo in Brookfield, Illinois, and published his findings in the journal *The American Naturalist*. He used model weasels of various sizes with and without black-tipped tails, and real red-tailed hawks that were trained to attack them.

Powell found that "long-tailed weasels with tail spots and least weasels with no spots were missed significantly more frequently by each hawk than the other color-size morphs." He also records that "observers occasionally noted that hawks attempted to grasp the tail of the long-tailed, tail-spot morph but were unable to hold the tail because of poor dexterity and tail thinness; or hawks appeared to check their attack and miss at the last moment as though they had been surprised by some aspect of the weasel model."[1]

The tail spot on the long-tailed and short-tailed weasels serves to deflect attacks away from vital organs. Deflection marks are common in insects (think about false eyes on butterfly wings or false heads on caterpillars), but not on other mammals (that we're aware of).

Wouldn't the least weasels, who lack tail spots, be at a disadvantage? Powell concluded that their small size makes it difficult for predators to see them in the first place, and with much shorter tails, the tail spot would be too close to vital organs for comfort.

Weasels' defensive strategies do not end with deflection marks and camouflage. Erratic movements, quick direction changes, and snow tunnels also help them evade predators. Lucky for me, all I need to catch is a glimpse of one weasel's tracks. Just that discovery gives me something satisfying to chew on as I glide up and over the next snow-covered hill.

American Martens

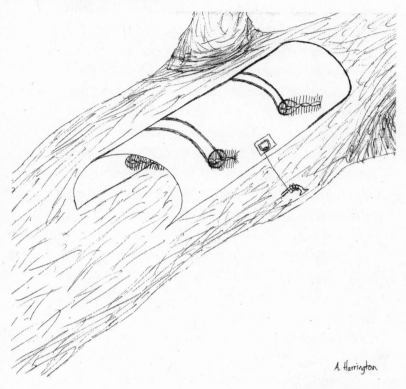

A. Harrington

Alan Harrington

The American marten (sometimes known as the pine marten) is the only mammal remaining on Wisconsin's state endangered species list. Even when they were more abundant, people rarely caught a glimpse of this shy, solitary, nocturnal weasel.

Until the 1920s American martens were widely distributed throughout the dense conifer and hardwood

woodlands of northern Wisconsin. Unregulated fur
harvest and habitat loss caused their demise. In 1986
a marten recovery plan was developed with the goal of
reestablishing two self-sustaining populations of martens
in the Chequamegon-Nicolet National Forest. But even
with cooperation between the Wisconsin DNR, the U.S.
Forest Service, and the Great Lakes Indian Fish and Wildlife
Commission (GLIFWC), marten populations in the
Chequamegon-Nicolet National Forest are not rebounding
as well as wildlife managers and researchers hoped.

Over a period of 15 years, 300 martens were released in
the Chequamegon-Nicolet National Forest with limited
success. Marten populations in the northeast part of the
release range have grown to about 220 animals and seem
to be holding their own. Unfortunately the number of
these mink-sized weasels in the Chequamegon side of the
forest appears to be lower.

Phil Manlick, a wildlife researcher and PhD student at
the UW–Madison, is studying martens in northwestern
Wisconsin. He has been gathering DNA samples from hair
traps to determine if the local martens are breeding with
reintroduced martens.

Phil and his research technician, Caroline, were staying
at the Museum's Jackson Burke House during their
winter field research period, so I tagged along on their
weekly trap line check to learn more. We skied about
10 kilometers in a morning, skimming along groomed
snowmobile trails north of Clam Lake. Using GPS units,

we navigated to the traps. After getting as close as possible on the snowmobile route, we removed our skis and slogged off road through deep snow to the trap location.

At each site Phil or Caroline dug the trap out from beneath a fallen log and checked to see if something had tripped it. The hair traps are homemade and consist of a wire brush fixed inside a PVC pipe about two feet long and five inches in diameter. The trap is baited with a little wire ball of food and squirt of strawberry jam. When an animal (usually a marten or another small weasel) goes in, it must pass by the wire brush to get the bait and again to exit. The researchers who designed the traps did not intend for them to capture live animals. Instead a wire brush just catches some hair, and that provides the DNA the researchers need.

By comparing the DNA of the hairs they capture to the DNA on record from every released marten, Phil will be able to tell if there has been any romance between the old and the new. Along with habitat and tracking data, this may help researchers tease out the reasons that martens aren't doing as well as we'd like.

With a slew of traits that prepare martens for survival in Northwoods winters, we would expect them to be plentiful. Small bodies and relatively large feet allow American martens to travel easily over snow. When the snow gets deep, martens tunnel through it to reach prey and to den in or under downed logs. These adaptations give martens an advantage over their competitors—bobcats, fishers, and red foxes. Not only do the adaptations help martens catch food, they prevent the martens from becoming food.

DNR wildlife biologist Jim Woodford explains, "Martens do better during years of high snowfalls in the north where they tunnel under snow in search of mice and other rodents. When there is less snowfall, as we have seen in the last few years, they are at a disadvantage."[2]

Unfortunately for martens, most climate change scenarios in the Northwoods predict reduced snow pack conditions. This would substantially decrease the advantage that big-footed/small-bodied martens have over other carnivores during winter and lead to lower numbers of martens. Aggression between martens, fishers, and other carnivores (like red foxes and bobcats) may increase as shallower snow allows the other animals to travel freely in winter.

Whatever challenges martens face, I'm rooting for them, and hoping to catch a glimpse of this rare and fascinating weasel.

Mythical Beasts

Elsa Hansen

"I was at ten thousand feet or so," began wildlife researcher Phil Manlick. "My friends were fishing on one side of an alpine lake, but I was sleeping and facing the other direction. I opened my eyes and saw a wolverine running across a snowfield on the north side of the canyon. First I gestured wildly, trying to get the group's attention. Then I yelled. They still didn't hear. One of the group members had been talking all week about how much he wanted to see a wolverine, so finally I shouted 'ALEX!' at the top of my lungs. Either the wolverine was named Alex," Phil jokes, "or I disturbed him a bit, because the large weasel stopped and looked at us. Then the wolverine turned and ran straight up over one of the highest passes in the Tetons, right into Idaho."

Phil has researched various animals all over the country, from elk and mule deer in Oregon to cougars and grizzly bears in Washington. He has tracked wolves in the Grand Tetons and now pine martens in Clam Lake, Wisconsin. But from the excitement that showed in his face, voice, and gestures as he shared this well-worn story, I could tell that this was a highlight of his animal encounters.

And it's no wonder. Wolverines are among the most elusive creatures on the planet and have become an almost mythical beast. As the largest land-dwelling member of the weasel family, wolverines take weasels' reputations for fierceness to the extreme. By some estimates, if a wolverine were the size of a bear, it would be the strongest creature on Earth. It is no exaggeration that the wolverine is the strongest animal of its size.

With this strength of body and will, wolverines live in some of the toughest terrain—the most rugged, remote, and fiercely raw—and can prey on large animals like deer, moose, bighorn sheep, and elk. Wolverines are opportunistic feeders who also eat carrion, smaller mammals, eggs, roots, and berries. Food in their harsh habitats can be scarce, so they have adapted to a feast-or-famine lifestyle by reportedly eating up to 40 pounds (their own body weight) at one time when food is available. This ability earned them the scientific name *Gulo gulo*, which means "glutton" in Latin.

Even rock-hard frozen food doesn't present a problem to wolverines, since they, like other mustelids, possess a special upper molar in the back of their mouth that is rotated ninety degrees, toward the inside of the mouth. This special characteristic allows wolverines to tear off meat from prey or carrion that has frozen solid.

This and other adaptations give wolverines an advantage in winter. Big, padded paws help them run over deep snow, and a relatively large, compact body with a thick, winter pelage minimizes heat loss. Their dark, oily fur is also highly hydrophobic, making it resistant to frost. Humans in many cultures have taken advantage of this trait by using the fur to line jackets and parkas. Scientists estimate that wolverines do not experience cold stress at even negative 40 degrees Fahrenheit.

Wolverines seem tough enough to withstand almost anything. And yet their population in the United States declined precipitously by the turn of the last century and is still declining today. Poisoned carcasses and fur trapping precipitated the initial decline. An entirely different set of stressors acts today.

Having snow cover through mid-May is essential to wolverine reproduction since females raise their kits in snow dens that provide protection from the cold and predators. Spring snow cover is the one element that all wolverine habitats across the continent have in common. Although Wisconsin has not had sufficient spring snow cover recently, scientists surmise that the Little Ice Age from 1350 to 1850 may have provided better habitat for wolverines in the Great Lakes region before accurate records were kept.

The distribution of current wolverine records in the contiguous United States is limited to north central Washington, northern and central Idaho, western Montana, and northwestern Wyoming, although rare sightings do still occur in the Great Lakes region. The wolverine was on Michigan's endangered species list until the late 1990s, when it was removed from the list because it wasn't expected to return.

Although the wolverine is a candidate for the federal endangered species list, its main threat is a warming climate, which is not a simple problem to address. The National Center for Atmospheric Research study found that "unless the wolverine is able to very rapidly adapt to summertime temperatures far above anything it currently experiences, and to a spring with little or no snow cover, it is unlikely that it will continue to survive in the contiguous U.S. under a high or medium-low carbon emissions scenario."[3]

The good news is that if we can reduce our emissions to the lowest emissions scenario, we can help these mythical beasts survive in the Tetons, not just in legends. Phil would appreciate that, and so would his friend Alex.

Maples on the Move

Laurel Finney

Late afternoon sun snuck out from under a cloud bank as my skis swished in the freshly groomed tracks. Days like this are the reason I love living in the Northwoods.

A slight breeze knocked loose days-old snow from where it had perched since the last big storm, and the white clumps fell from branches and twigs with soft plops that were more visual than auditory. The motion drew my eyes up, and I took a moment to appreciate the woods. This section of the Valhalla ski trail, off County Road C near Washburn, Wisconsin, climbs through an even-age stand of deciduous trees.

The dark, furrowed bark of aspen graded to creamy white in the canopy. Paper birches with dying tops still presented pure white bark at eye level. The most common trees had the smooth, brownish-gray bark of young maples, and a quick look at winter buds on the saplings told me that this forest holds both red and sugar maples.

Red maples have been a favorite of mine since my college botany class when I appreciated the crimson color of their twigs and buds that make them easy to identify. Autumn reinforces my appreciation of *Acer rubrum*, as I watch their leaves flash a brilliant rainbow of green, yellow, orange, and red all on the same tree.

I also admire their resilience. I've seen them in some of the harshest habitats available: from swamps to droughty soils, in bedrock crevasses and on spongy beds of decaying organic matter, on mountainsides with the toughest firs, and in soggy creek bottoms tangled with alders. Red maples are one of the most abundant and widespread tree species in eastern North America and have the widest tolerance to climatic conditions of all the North American species of maple. And they are becoming more common.

An increase in winter temperatures has given the green light for red maples to move north into territory where they would previously have been killed by extreme cold. Current fire suppression policies also favor red maple, which does not do well with repeated fires, but can respond vigorously after a single fire by sprouting rapidly from dormant buds on the root crown. Seedling establishment can occur from surviving trees onsite or helicopter seeds carried in on the wind.

While red maple is susceptible to numerous pathogens, fire, and damage by sapsuckers, climate change might thwart one of its leaf diseases. A Duke University study revealed that infections of a certain fungus were less common and less severe in red maples exposed to higher-than-normal concentrations of atmospheric carbon dioxide.

I am happy that red maples seem to have a secure place in the uncertain future of our forests, but the coming changes might not be beneficial for its cousin the sugar maple. Researchers at the University of Wisconsin– Madison predict that sugar maples will decline in Wisconsin. Increasing winter temperatures are causing stress and escalating insect damage. Warmer springs are making the sugaring season shorter, smaller, and less predictable. Although red maple can be tapped for making syrup, its season is frustratingly short. Red maple flowers much earlier than sugar maple, and the sap becomes unpalatable after bud break.

Buds were still clasped tightly against the cold on this February day, but I was warm from a long climb. As I reached the top of a hill and rounded a corner, the forest changed. A rosy sunset glowed through the heavy bows of balsam firs. I pushed off with my poles to gain momentum and went whizzing through a gnarled stand of oaks. A sharp corner forced me to step out of the tracks, but I kept my balance and savored the wind in my face, soon gliding into a cathedral of pines. Glimpses of the sky showed that it was still painted with a full palate of pinks.

A world in motion may be confusing, and sharp turns in the path may throw us off balance. Change often means losing as well as gaining. Sometimes we might rather just stand still and savor a particular place and a particular moment. Though change will never end, we can help guide its direction and strive to find beauty in every shifting hue.

Magical Things

Elsa Hansen

I am constantly amazed by how much I do not know about the world. As the English author Eden Phillpotts says, "The universe is full of magical things patiently waiting for our wits to grow sharper."⁴

My wits have just recently sharpened enough to discover that common redpolls, those brown-streaked, red-foreheaded finches, are not as common as I'd thought. If you feed the birds, you've probably noticed sizable flocks of redpolls moving frenetically, foraging determinedly, and then swirling away at the slightest thing. You have likely observed that they prefer tiny thistle or nyjer seeds.

This is an example of the specialized beaks of the finch family. Darwin's finches are the classic model for this, with beaks that are quite varied in order to be highly adapted to their diverse food sources. Other local examples include crossbills, who are finches with curved bills that can pry open tightly closed spruce cones, and rose-breasted grosbeaks, who have robust, cone-shaped beaks that can crack bigger seeds and catch larger insects.

The tiny beaks of the redpolls are much better suited for delicate thistle seeds than they are for hearty sunflower seeds. When not at your feeder, redpolls feast on the tiny seeds of birches, alders, willows, spruces, pines, grasses, buttercups, and mustards. In warm weather they eat quite a few small insects and spiders.

Birches, willows, and spruces grow farther north than most other trees, so it makes sense that redpolls, who breed in the taiga and tundra, prefer their seeds. Food is not the only issue when you are a circumpolar species, though. This is where they get especially interesting. I just learned that redpolls can survive temperatures of *negative* 65 degrees Fahrenheit. That's cold!

Redpolls have several physiological and behavioral adaptations to living in the cold. First they increase their insulation. Just like you dig your down jacket out of the closet each fall, redpolls grow about 31 percent more feathers by November. Then redpolls take a hint from the subnivean creatures—they sometimes tunnel into the snow to stay warm during long winter nights. Their tunnels can be over a foot long and four inches under the surface. That is impressive for such a tiny bird!

Redpolls share a behavioral adaptation with another subnivean resident, too. Just like chipmunks stuffing their cheeks full of seeds, redpolls have a pocket in their neck, called an esophageal diverticulum, where they can store seeds. The extra seeds allow them to "feed" while huddling in a protected place, overnight, or during a storm. These seeds fuel the birds' metabolism, and allow them to maintain their body temperature.

Enjoy watching these gregarious flocks of finches while you can! Soon they will swirl away north to their breeding grounds. Although we are happy to see 10, 20, or 100 in our yard, their global population is estimated in the tens of millions. Yes, the universe really is full of magical things.

A Crappie Evening

Ryan Nechuta, age 6

First my car got stuck on the snow-covered lake. Then the truck got stuck, too. After much ado, with the car sitting back at the landing on solid ground, and everyone squashed into the truck, we reached the honey hole.

Leaden skies hung low over the snow covered lake. Two other ice fishing houses sat just off the pine-treed point as we parked the truck at the third point of the triangle. Out came the sled with the pop-up shelter. Out came the five-gallon pails filled with rods and holders, ice scoops, and minnows. The power auger growled to life, and soon we had nine holes, six tip-downs, three people keeping watch, and three people jigging.

"The crappies start biting at four o'clock," said Larry, our friend and fishing guide, as he slipped the last hook under the dorsal fin of a crappie minnow.

3:58 . . . 4:00 . . . 4:02 . . . 4:04 . . . "There's one!" someone shouted as the pole in the rod stand tipped down. Mom quickly grabbed the pole and set the hook. Hand over mittened hand, she pulled up the line until the brilliant scales of a black crappie slid out of the hole and onto the snow. Right on schedule.

The next fish got away, though, as a rusty angler (who will remain nameless) tried to pull it straight up out of the hole. Also known as "papermouths," crappies have tender mouths that can't support their own weight, and a hook will pull out easily.

After that, I kept busy watching the other tip-downs, delivering crappie minnows into waiting hands and scooping ice from the holes as the water skimmed over. Running through deep snow in my clunky boots, I felt like a little kid. The three holes closest to deep water were the most successful, presumably since the hungry crappies encountered these first as they moved from the depths of the main lake into the shallows off our point.

Black crappies prefer habitats with little or no current, clear water, and abundant cover. Schools of crappies find shelter in plants and underwater structures, such as logs, stumps, and rocks. Crappies feed some early in the morning, but wait until this dusky hour to have their main course. Smaller crappies eat plankton and small crustaceans while larger fish eat insects, crustaceans, small fish, and minnows. Their predators include larger fish, great blue herons, snapping turtles, kingfishers, and of course, anglers.

With shimmering, light green scales densely patterned with dark spots, and rows of more dark spots on their fins, this colorful and plentiful member of the sunfish family is a popular game fish. While their original range was likely confined to the eastern United States and Canada, black crappies now inhabit all of the lower 48 states.

It was not even 5 o'clock when I dumped the fish bucket out onto the snow to count our haul. "Seventeen . . . eighteen . . . nineteen . . . we just need one more to make twenty!" Freezing rain was pelting our backs, and we took turns brushing the skim of ice off each other's jackets. The biting wind began to steal our inner warmth, but we were determined to reach this arbitrary goal.

Larry started to pack up the shallowest tip-downs that were not catching anything. I took the pole from my friend when he decided to crawl into the clamshell tent with the propane heater to warm up. Up and down. Up and down. I pulled the line high enough to make sure that the minnow was still alive, and tried to make sense of the red flashes on the fish finder. I think I was more focused on trying to jig correctly than on actually catching anything when my bobber bobbed. With a little yank and a yell, I set the hook and hauled up our final fish.

The faint odor of fish slime rose from our mittens as the truck heater warmed up. We bounced and jostled back onto the shore, heading toward our dinner. In the back of the truck was a pail of beautiful fish whose dinner we had interrupted. Some days it sure is good to be part of the food chain!

Shrike!

Susan Lewis

Heavy snow brought a carnival of birds to our feeders. Starting at 6:57 a.m., with a black-capped chickadee, there was a steady stream of goldfinches, redpolls, red- and white-breasted nuthatches, blue jays, and even a hairy woodpecker. It was fun to watch as the tiny birds flew in and out of caves in the snow-laden branches of the hemlock trees. Sometimes we could see a little flake of snow stuck to a chickadee's head or caught in the whiskers around its bill.

Then, in a flash of feathers, they were gone.

The reason for their quick retreat landed on top of the snow pile. Sporting a black bandit mask on his gray head, this Northern Shrike looked the part of a feathered villain.

Surprisingly, this skilled predator is a songbird. Being songbirds, shrikes lack the sharp talons of raptors like hawks and owls. Being songbirds, shrikes have another weapon. Like the winged Sirens of Greek mythology, shrikes sing sweetly to attract other songbirds. Once prey is lured in, shrikes attack with a solid blow, then finish the job by biting the neck, shaking, or repeated knocks to the skull with their sharp beak. Shrikes often kill more prey than they need right away and impale the leftovers on long thorns or barbed wire. Impaling prey on thorns may seem brutal, but it is just a practical way to compensate for having delicate feet that cannot grip food during dinner.

The stored prey also provides the shrike with food security and will eventually get eaten when the hunting is poor. A male shrike with abundant prey impaled throughout his territory has a better chance of attracting mates and fathering successful nests. Breeding takes place north of 50 degrees latitude around the globe. In winter shrikes migrate only as far as necessary to find food, which often means they come to Wisconsin. The visitor at my bird feeder should be on his way back home soon, to begin courtship in March or April.

In the meantime, I hope he is finding enough to eat. (While I love my chickadees, I am an equal-opportunity bird feeder.) More than half of a shrike's diet is small rodents like mice and voles. Unfortunately, those tasty little critters are safely hiding beneath a foot of snow in the subnivean layer. While foxes and owls have enough mass to break through the crust and dig for tunneling mice, shrikes do not have that ability. Thus, songbirds are a larger part of their diet now, as well as in early spring when male songbirds are distracted by courtship, and in late summer when fledglings are an easy catch. Insects, frogs, toads, and salamanders round out a shrike's diet.

The carnival of seed-eating songbirds took their sweet time returning to my feeders. They seemed a little more skittish and a bit more vigilant as we all scanned the treetops for another glimpse of our thrilling winter visitor.

Saying My Last Goodbyes

orientation ↑

Mimi Crandall

Early spring is a marvelous time. The Sun's rays are intense enough to melt ice despite air temperatures that hover near zero. The pussy willow buds are opening, despite blustery weather and forecasts for more snow. Even the buds on the oak trees are starting to swell. Not long ago, I encountered the first skunk wandering hungrily out of his winter sleep. Every beautiful afternoon teases me into thinking about bicycling and gardening.

Yet I feel like I am saying my last goodbyes after a long visit with an old friend. Every time I ski a trail, I wonder, "Will this be the last time I ski this trail this year?" The animals are feeling spring fever, too, and as they wander farther and faster on the thick crust of the snow, they leave behind a maze of tracks. I also feel sentimental about these, since summer tracking is confined to sandy or muddy edges and those rare soft soils not covered by life.

So I think, "Is this the last weasel track I'll see for the winter? I had better stop a moment and admire the incredible length of its jumps one more time." "Are these the last fox tracks I'll see, trotting daintily down the ski tracks and leaving musky scent marks on baby balsam trees?" Maybe I won't even see many more squirrel tracks, although they seem to persist the longest and pattern every last snow pile with their four-toed front feet and five-toed back feet.

In this transitional season I make sure to savor every moment left of winter. On a recent ski through a friend's young woods, grouse feet quilted the crusty snow in lines and loops and spirals. Their tracks went winding around, under, and through the bare, twiggy shrubs. Projections on the sides of the grouse's four toes, grown just for winter, worked like snowshoes to keep them afloat.

Suddenly a blur of dark brown rose from the edge of the trail. I had followed the tracks right to the grouse! It must have landed recently because the grouse's trail was short. It began just a couple feet off the ski trail with a sitzmark. Most of us up here think of a sitzmark (one of my favorite words) as an impression made in the snow by a skier falling backward. But I first encountered this term in animal tracking vocabulary, referring to the mark made by the belly flop of a mouse or a squirrel as they dive off a tree into deep snow.

The grouse's sitzmark was an impression of its belly from a soft landing. A chain of maybe a hundred footsteps led up the bank and into the woods, then ended with an elegant pattern of wing marks where the grouse took flight again.

Soon the grouse will be drumming up love. Soon the snow will be all melted. Soon I will only be able to find tracks along the lakeshore in soft sand. During some years at this time it has been 75 degrees with the ice out, boats in the water, violets blooming, maple and poplar buds popping, spring peepers peeping, maple sugaring season come and gone, and even the lilac buds bursting. Some years, I've still been skiing in April. You can always count on nature to be unpredictable.

Although I love winter and try to savor every last bit of skiable, trackable snow, soon the momentum of spring will take over. Each new bit of bare dirt, each swelling bud, each returning bird will push the memories of skiing through restful black-and-white woods further back in my memory. Soon, if you ask me which season is my favorite,

I may pause for a moment from planting seeds, or smelling a flower, or spying on a warbler. "Why spring, of course!" I'll say, as I tilt my head back in the sunshine and look to the sky.

Notes

SPRING

The Breeze of Balance

1. Hugh Raffles, *Insectopedia* (New York: Pantheon Books, 2010), 7.

Maple Syrup

2. Bernd Heinrich, "Maple Sugaring by Red Squirrels," *Journal of Mammalogy* vol. 73, no. 1 (Oxford University Press, 1992), 51–54. DOI:10.2307/1381865.

3. Michael J. Caduto, "Yellow-Bellied Sapsuckers Provide Food for Many Species," *Northern Woodlands* (July 11, 2011). Accessed March 2, 2016, http://northernwoodlands.org/outside_story /article/yellow-bellied-sapsuckers-provide-food-for-many-species.

Change

4. Jennifer A. Francis and Stephen J. Vavrus, "Evidence Linking Arctic Amplification to Extreme Weather in Mid-latitudes," *Geophysical Research Letters,* vol. 39, no. 6 (March 17, 2012). DOI:10.1029/2012GL051000.

5. Chuck Quirmbach, "Arctic Ice Decline Could Be Cause of Frigid March," *Wisconsin Public Radio*, March 27, 2013. Accessed March 2, 2016, http://www.wpr.org/arctic-ice-decline -could-be-cause-frigid-march.

Little Packets of Fatty Goodness

6. Régis Ferriere, Judith L. Bronstein, Sergio Rinaldi, Richard Law, Mathias Gauduchon, "Cheating and the Evolutionary Stability of Mutualisms," Proceedings of the Royal Society of London B (April 22, 2002) 269, 773–780. Accessed March 2, 2016, DOI:10.1098/rspb.2001.1900.

Salamanders and the Sun

7. R. Kerney, E. Kim, R. P. Hangarter, A. A. Heiss, C. D. Bishop and B. K. Hall (2011), "Intracellular Invasion of Green Algae in a Salamander Host," Proceedings of the National Academy of Sciences USA 108: 6497–6502. http://www.pnas.org /content/108/16/6497.short. Accessed March 2, 2016.

A Delight for the Senses

8. http://www.smokymountainnews.com/component/k2/ item/10276-some-scarlet-tanagers-are-orange.

The Smell of Rain

9. Isabel Joy Bear and Roderick G. Thomas, "Nature of Argillaceous Odour," *Nature* 201 (March 1964). (4923): 993–995. DOI:10.1038/201993a0.

SUMMER

Little White Flowers

1. J. Edwards, D. Witaker, S. Klionsky and M. J. Laskowski, "A Record-breaking Pollen Catapult," *Nature* 435 (May 12, 2005), 164.

Magic on the River

2. Sigurd Olson, *The Singing Wilderness* (University of Minnesota Press, 1956), 82–83.
3. Ibid., 83.
4. Aldo Leopold, *A Sand County Almanac: And Sketches Here and There* (Oxford University Press, 1949), 157–158.
5. Olson, *The Singing Wilderness*, 83.

Mosquitoes

6. Jittawadee Murphy, "Ecology: A World without Mosquitoes," *Nature* 466, 432–434 (2010). DOI:10.1038/466432a. Accessed March 2, 2016,
   http://www.nature.com/news/2010/100721/full/466432a. html.

7. Bruce Harrison, "Ecology: A World without Mosquitoes," *Nature* 466, 432–434 (2010). DOI:10.1038/466432a. Accessed March 2, 2016,
http://www.nature.com/news/2010/100721/full/466432a.html.

Kale: Servant or Master

8. Michael Pollan, *The Botany of Desire: A Plant's-Eye View of the World*, (New York: Random House, 2001).
9. Ibid.
10. Ibid.
11. Ibid.

Web of Intrigue

12. Nadia Drake, "Why Male Dark Fishing Spiders Spontaneously Die after Sex," *Wired* (June 19, 2013). Accessed March 2, 2016, http://www.wired.com/2013/06/spider-sex.

In a Field of Goldenrod: Part II

13. Edwin Way Teale, quoted in "An Unbelievably Galling Report," *Niagra This Week,* December 31, 2010. Accessed March 2, 2016, http://www.niagarathisweek.com/opinion-story/3259218-an-unbelievably-galling-report.

FALL

A Dandelion Smile

1. Thich Nhat Hanh, *Peace Is Every Step: The Path of Mindfulness in Everyday Life* (New York: Bantam, 1992), 22–23.
2. "Tech Helps Dandelions Ooze," *Discovery News* (February 11, 2013). Accessed March 2, 2016, http://news.discovery.com/tech/dandelion-latex.htm.

WINTER

Predator and Prey

1. Roger A. Powell, "Evolution of Black-Tipped Tails in Weasels: Predator Confusion," *The American Naturalist,* Vol. 119, No. 1 (January 1982), 126–131. Accessed March 2, 2016, http://repository.lib.ncsu.edu/publications/bitstream/1840.2/537/1/Powell_1982_american.

American Martens

2. Wisconsin Department of Natural Resources, "American Marten Research Shows Rare Mammal Benefits from Heavy Snowfall," April 8, 2008. Accessed March 2, 2016, http://dnr.wi.gov/news/weekly/weeklynews_print.asp?id=675.

Mythical Beasts

3. National Science Foundation, "Wolverines Threatened by Climate Change, Earlier Springs," (February 3, 2011). Accessed March 2, 2016, https://www.nsf.gov/news/news_summ.jsp?cntn_id=118543.

Magical Things

4. Eden Phillpotts, *A Shadow Passes* (New York: The Macmillan Company, 1919). http://quoteinvestigator.com/2012/07/07/magical-things-waiting.

Note about illustrations:

Illustrations for this book were truly a community effort. Since kids are often the inspiration for Natural Connections articles, the Cable Natural History Museum conducted an art contest for local students to illustrate each of the chapters. The hope was that students would read some chapters, learn something about the plants and animals in those chapters, do a little more research on their own, and then create a black-and-white line drawing based on their research. We were thrilled with the response. To fill in the gaps, the Museum opened up the illustration project to artists of all ages and abilities. Friends, relatives, strangers, amateurs and professionals were all tapped to translate Emily's writing into simple drawings. Many thanks to all who contributed to this project!

Note about proceeds:

Proceeds from this book will support natural history education for youth at the Cable Natural History Museum.

Mimi Crandall

Acknowledgments

Everything in nature is connected. Nothing is created without the support of a zillion other living and nonliving parts of the Universe. This book is no different. It could not be in existence without the trees in the paper; the sources of energy used to write, print, and transport the final product; and the Earth that sustains us all.

Of course, many humans contributed their talents as well. I won't list them all here, but they know who they are. My parents, Margaret and Larry Stone, deserve much credit for bestowing on me their book- and nature-loving genes, for raising a mud-and-water-daughter, for using lots of red pen and encouragement on my high school papers, for continuing to edit my newspaper articles each week, and for immeasurable support in every way imaginable. My brother and sister-in-law contributed four fantastic children to the family, who provide me with much joy and inspiration.

My esteemed teachers, Mrs. Moser, Mrs. Probert, Mrs. Stott, and Mrs. Gnagy, all made learning the nuts and bolts of English quite enjoyable. Rick Penn, my grizzled, curmudgeonly, English 211 professor at Northland College gave me, for the first time, the delightful assignment of a short essay due every week. He had wonderful taste in books. Professor Alan Brew did as well. Many natural history professors, especially Craig Prudhomme, ignited my spark for interpreting the natural world. Tom Fitz, Jim Meeker, and Mike Link fleshed out those ideas, as did all the brilliant professors and fellow students in the Field Naturalist and Ecological Planning master's programs at the University of Vermont.

I am also grateful to the Cable Natural History Museum community, led by energetic Museum Director Deb Nelson, for their support. The Museum's founding director, Lois Nestel, started a tradition with her Wayside Wanderings newspaper articles, which Sue (Benson) Thurn continued enthusiastically. I'm honored to receive the torch from those remarkable women. Without a weekly assignment to compose a newspaper column, I probably wouldn't find the time to write at all. Without the positive comments from readers, I would surely burn out. Without the twenty or more newspapers willing to carry my column, I wouldn't have such a wide audience. Thanks also to the kids (of all ages) who ask great questions and inspire me with their curiosity.

From within the Museum community, several people— Fred Stratton, Jodi and Henry Kingdon, and Ron and Patty Anderson—have generously supported this project financially as well as with kind words and shared excitement. Everyone who supports the Museum is part of this book. Thanks to all of the artists, young and old, who participated in my crazy idea and helped me illustrate this book with their wonderful and whimsical drawings. I'm so glad to have you involved.

Kathi Dunn and Hobie Hobart of Dunn and Associates, and copy editor Susan Niemi helped make the idea a

ACKNOWLEDGMENTS

reality though their wisdom and professional experience. Although many have helped, I assure you that any errors still remaining are my own.

And again, thanks to the natural world, who provides a constant source of inspiration, connection, and mystery.